LET'S SPEAK KOREAN:
1,400+ EXPRESSIONS & 21 TOPICS
W/ PRONUNCIATION & GRAMMAR GUIDE MARKS FOR QUICK AND E

ISBN 979-11-88195-46-6

FANDOM MEDIA

Table of Contents

For audio files, please visit :

newampersand.com/SPEAKKOREAN

Hello everyone! Welcome to Let's Speak Korean! As you can see from my facial expression, I'm so excited to help you learn the most essential expressions in the Korean language!

Whether you are a K-Pop/K-Drama fanatic or just someone trying to pick up some useful expressions before going on a trip to Korea, this book surely will be a great resource!

This book, which contains **over 1,400 expressions from 21 different topics and situations**, is designed in a way that anyone with no knowledge in Korean can learn and use right away, **through simply listening and repeating** the expressions.

To help expedite the learning process and get you up to speed, we've created a **dedicated web page with downloadable/streaming audio files** where you can listen to each and every expression, recorded by a native Korean speaker - you get to hear how each syllable is pronounced, eliminating any unnecessary guesswork. I mean, you don't want to embarrass yourself by saying something that's totally inaccurate, right?

11 아니요, 몰라요. / 네, 알아요.
   a-ni-yo, mol-la-yo. / ne, al-a-yo.

No, I don't know. / Yes, I do know.

Not only that, you will find that every expression has **a romanized version underneath a corresponding Korean expression, with different types of guide marks which clearly teaches which means which in a given sentence.** With this, you won't be left alone in the dark, wondering where in the world you are.

While our goal is to help you learn to speak the expressions without having to study the Korean language itself, there are some basic stuff that will come up repeatedly, so it's worth getting to know them now because it will help you further understand how Korean language is structured. So without any further ado, let's go ahead and get started!

How To Read And Pronounce The Korean Alphabet

Play The Audio File "Consonats.mp3"

	Name	Pronunciation Initial / Final	English Approximation	Korean Example
ㄱ	기역 gi-yŏk	g / k	good	가수 gasu
ㄲ	쌍기역 ssang gi-yŏk	kk / k	skin	꿈 kkum
ㄴ	니은 ni-ŭn	n / n	nano	노루 noru
ㄷ	디귿 di-gŭt	d / t	dog	다리 dari
ㄸ	쌍디귿 ssang di-gŭt	dd	stall	땀 ddam
ㄹ	리을 ri-ŭl	r / l	roman	라면 ramyŏn
ㅁ	미음 mi-ŭm	m / m	man	마법 mabŏp
ㅂ	비읍 bi-ŭp	b / p	bean	보배 bobae
ㅃ	쌍비읍 ssang bi-ŭp	bb	spit	빨리 bbali
ㅅ	시옷 si-ot	s / t	sing	소리 sori
ㅆ	쌍시옷 ssang si-ot	ss	see	싸움 ssaum
ㅇ	이응 i-ŭng	silent / ng	vowel sound	아기 agi
ㅈ	지읒 ji-ŭt	j / t	jam	자유 jayu
ㅉ	쌍지읒 ssang ji-ŭt	jj	hats	짬뽕 jjamppong
ㅊ	치읓 chi-ŭt	ch / t	change	최고 choego
ㅋ	키읔 ki-ŭk	k / k	king	커피 kŏpi
ㅌ	티읕 ti-ŭt	t / t	time	타자 taja
ㅍ	피읖 pi-ŭp	p / p	prize	피로 piro
ㅎ	히읗 hi-ŭt	h / t	home	해변 haebyŏn

Korean alphabet consists of 14 consonants and 10 vowels. The ones in gray are special ones - these consonants are called tense consonants, and are said with a harder, stiffer sound.

Keep in mind that there are no English/Roman letters that perfectly describe the sounds.

But don't worry - listen to the audio files and keep practicing and you will start hearing the differences!

Are you wondering what it means by "**Initial / Final**" pronunciation? Don't worry! It's not as difficult as it may sound. We'll get to the bottom of it after we cover the vowels.

	Pronunciation	English Approximation	Korean Example
ㅏ	a	grandpa	자두 jadu
ㅑ	ya	see-ya	야구 yagu
ㅓ	ŏ	up	접시 jŏpsi
ㅕ	yŏ	young	명화 myŏnghwa
ㅗ	o	go	고무 gomu
ㅛ	yo	yogurt	교사 gyosa
ㅜ	u	root	우주 uju
ㅠ	yu	you	소유 soyu
ㅡ	ŭ	good	그림 gŭrim
ㅣ	i	hit	소리 sori
ㅔ	e	energy	세기 segi
ㅐ	ae	tablet	대박 daebak
ㅒ	yae	yes	얘기 yaegi
ㅖ	ye	yes	예복 yebok
ㅙ	oae	where	안돼 andwae
ㅞ	ue	quest	훼손 hweson
ㅚ	oe	wet	최고 choego

Play The Audio File "Vowels.mp3"

And the vowels in gray are called diphthongs, or complex vowels, meaning "double vowels". They are made up of two vowels to create one sound.

One thing you might have noticed is how ㅐ/ㅔ practically sound the same and ㅚ / ㅙ / ㅞ the same!

It might look like a waste of ink, but their meanings differ when written.

Until the late 20th century, people used to distinguish the minute differences coming from the tongue and mouth position, but the differences in technique are seldom observed nowadays, and most Koreans can't tell one apart from another.

While ㅚ is ㅗ + ㅣ so "oi" seems right when followed the rules,			
but it's pronounced as "oe", and it's not considered a "double vowel", either.			
ㅘ	wa	what	과일 gwail
ㅟ	wi	wisconsin	귀 gwi
ㅢ	ŭi	we	의자 ŭija
ㅝ	wŏ	wonder	견투 gwontu

Korean alphabets are then put together to create a **syllable block**, which is composed of a **beginning consonant**, a **middle/final vowel**, and an **optional final consonant**, known as **batchim**. In order to create a syllable block, you need at least one consonant and one vowel. Let's take a look at the example below.

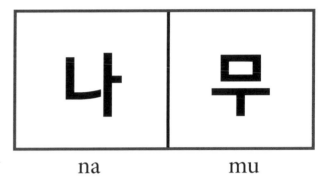

na   mu

Here is an example.

나무 (na mu), meaning "tree".
Let's look at how the word is structured.

consonant

vowel

consonant   vowel

As you can see, a syllable block is composed of a consonant and a vowel. At this point, you might have noticed the position of a vowel is different on the two syllables.

ㅏ	ㅑ	ㅓ	ㅕ	ㅐ	ㅣ	ㅒ	ㅖ	ㅖ
아	야	어	여	애	이	얘	에	예

The 9 vowels above are positioned **to the right side of** a consonant.
When a vowel is spoken by itself, ㅇ, which is silent, is always placed as a place holder.

ㅗ	ㅛ	ㅜ	ㅠ	ㅡ	ㅚ	ㅟ	ㅢ	ㅘ	ㅝ	ㅙ	ㅞ
오	요	우	유	으	외	위	의	와	워	왜	웨

The 12 vowels above are positioned **below** a consonant. Just try to memorize them for now.

4

As promised, let's talk about **final consonants**, or **batchim.** Simply put, they are the very last consonant character of a word ending in a consonant. For example, the word **"good"** has a final consonant of **"d"**, while the word **"Korean"** has a final consonant of **"n"**. The word **"language"**, however, **does not** have a final consonant because it ends with a vowel. Korean is just the same. See the following to understand better.

ggum
("dream")

consonant
vowel
final consonant

As you can see, the ㅁ comes at the bottom to serve as a final consonant. Notice the vowel ㅜ is placed underneath the consonant ㄲ.

This is the rule we learned just a page ago ;)

Let's take a look at another example to practice.

bap
("meal")

consonant   vowel

final consonant

In this case, the vowel ㅏ is placed to the right side of a consonant ㅂ, and the final consonant ㅂ is placed underneath the vowel. This is what it looks like.

It's easier to remember like this : **the final consonant is always placed underneath a vowel**, whether the vowel is the right side-type vowel or the underneath type-vowel. Oh, and the word **batchim** literally means "to support/hold up", so just picture it holding a consonant and a vowel ;)

so
("cow")

consonant
vowel

As a reminder, a syllable that ends in a vowel alone **does not need a final consonant, or batchim.**

At this point, you might be wondering why the same consonant ㅂ, are represented with different alphabet (**b** and **p**). Remember the alphabet chart? We told you that the consonants can be used as a **final consonant/batchim,** and they are pronounced differently when they do. See the chart on the next page.

Consonant	Name	First Consonant Pronunciation	Final Consonant Pronunciation	Example			When Followed By A Vowel		When Followed By A Vowel ㅣ [i]
ㄱ	gi-yŏk	g		책	book	chaek	책이	chaeg-i	
ㅋ	ki-ŭk	k	k	부엌	kitchen	buŏk			
ㄲ	ssang gi-yŏk	gg		깎다	to carve	ggak da	깎아	ggagg-a	
ㄴ	ni-ŭn	n	n	손	hand	son			
ㄷ	di-gŭt	d		곧다	straight	got da	곧아	god-a	go-ji
ㅌ	ti-ŭt	t		끝	end	ggŭt	끝에	ggŭt-e	ggŭ-chi
ㅅ	si-ot	s		옷	clothes	ot	옷이	os-i	
ㅆ	ssang shi-ot	ss	t	있다	there is	it da	있어	iss-ŏ	
ㅈ	ji-ŭt	j		찾다	to find	chat da	찾아	chaj-a	
ㅊ	chi-ŭt	ch		꽃	flower	ggot	꽃이	ggoch-i	
ㅎ	hi-ŭt	h		넣다	to put in	nŏt da			
ㄹ	ri-ŭl	r	l	말	horse	mal			
ㅁ	mi-ŭm	m	m	솜	cotton	som			
ㅂ	bi-up	b		입	mouth	ip	입이	ib-i	
ㅍ	pi-ŭp	p	p	잎	leaf	ip	잎이	ip-i	
ㅇ	i-ŭng	silent	ng	콩	bean	kong			

Looking at the above chart will help you visually understand how a consonant is pronounced differently, when used as a **first consonant** and **final consonant,** or **batchim.** Note that the colored consonants **retain** their **original first consonant sound** when followed by a vowel. Just think of it this way - a syllable made up of only a vowel always has a ㅇ as a placeholder (we learned this). So, the final consonant of a syllable right before that comes in place of the placeholder. You only need to remember the colored ones.

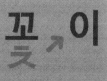

Now let's get ready to learn the expressions! In order to have a smooth launch, let's familiarize yourself with some of the elements that will keep popping up repeatedly.

First, Korean sentences are structured in the following format.

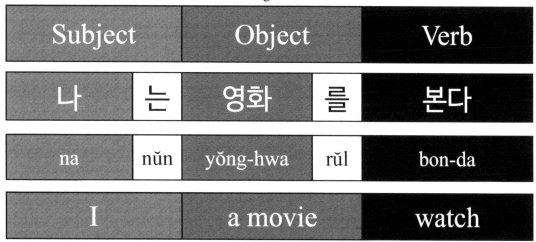

Subject		Object		Verb
나	는	영화	를	본다
na	nŭn	yŏng-hwa	rŭl	bon-da
I		a movie		watch

As you can see, Korean sentences are structured in a different order than English sentences. It should look awkward at this moment, but you will get used to it as we practice more. Another thing you should have noticed is the "는" that comes right after the subject and "를" which comes immediately after the object and an object, left uncolored (we did it on purpose). You will also see that there is no English translation for them, and it's because there aren't any words that correspond to them directly.

This is quite similar to the concept of a/the of English grammar, something that can't be translated directly into Korean, but we know what they are and what they do. Oh, so what are they in Korean?

They are called, **"topic marker (은/는)"** and **"subject marker (이/가)"**

Topic Marker

> 은 (ŭn) : **Used after a word ending with a final consonant.**
> **Ex.) 몸 mom, "body" + 은**
>
> 는 (nŭn) : **Used after a word ending with a vowel.**
> **Ex.) 나 na, "I" + 는**

The main role of a topic marker is to indicate what's being talked about (i.e., "topic"), or will be talked about. Although there is no direct translation, you can think of it as meaning "as for".

For example,

> **하늘은 높다. ha-nŭl-ŭn nop-da : As for the sky, it's high.**
> *하늘 – sky / 높다 – high
>
> **그녀는 학생입니다. gŭ-nyŏ-nŭn hak-saeng-ip-ni-da : As for her, she's a student.**
> *그녀 – she / 학생 – student

Subject Marker

이 (i) : Used after a word ending with a final consonant.
Ex.) 손 son, "hand" + 이

가 (ga) : Used after a word ending with a vowel.
Ex.) 새 sae, "bird" + 가

In a similar fashion, a **subject marker** comes after a subject to indicate **what the subject of the sentence is**.

For example,

가격이 얼마죠? ga-gyŏg-i ŏl-ma-jyo? : How much is the price?
*가격 – price / 얼마 – how much

자동차가 멈췄다. ja-dong-cha-ga mŏm-chwŏt-da. :The car stopped.
*자동차 – car / 멈췄다 – stopped

Below are some samples from our expressions you will be learning later on. Identify where they are used and try to get used to their usage and nuance.

01 제 이름은 김철수입니다.
je i-rŭm-ŭn kim-chŏl-su-ip-ni-da.
My name is Kim Cheol-soo.

24 저는 학생입니다.
jŏ-nŭn hak-saeng-ip-ni-da.
I'm a student.

48 수업이 취소되었어요.
(su-ŏb-i chwi-so-doe-ŏ-ssŏ-yo.)
The class has been canceled.

57 게이트가 몇번인가요?
ge-i-tŭ-ga myŏt-bŏn-in-ga-yo?
What number is the gate?

Now that we covered the concept of **topic marker** and **subject marker**, it's time to talk about **"을"** and **"를"**, which comes right after the object of a sentence. If you're quick-witted (I'm 100% sure you are!), then you might have guessed the name of this element. Right! It's called the **object marker**!

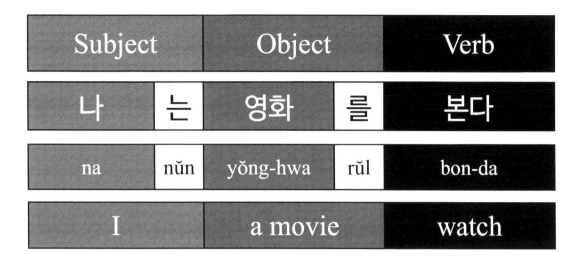

Object Marker

> 을 (ŭl) : **Used after a word ending with a final consonant.**
> **Ex.)** 수박 su-bak, "watermelon" + 을
>
> 를 (rŭl) : **Used after a word ending with a vowel.**
> **Ex.)** 두부 du-bu, "tofu" + 를

Object markers in Korean sentences signify that a noun is acting as the object of the sentence. For syllables ending in a final consonant, use 을, and syllables ending with a vowel, use 를 .

For example,

> **음악을 듣는다. ŭm-ak-ŭl dŭt-nŭn-da : (I) listen to music.**
> *음악 – music / 듣는다 – to listen
>
> **김치를 먹는다. kim-chi-rŭl mŏk-nŭn-da : I eat Kimchi**
> *먹는다 – to eat

In colloquial speech, though, they are often dropped when the sentence object is obvious from the context.

While it's a very confusing/difficult concept for non-Koreans, you shouldn't worry too much about it because Korean people will still understand what you are trying to say even if you mix them up, or forget to use them! Just listen to a lot of Korean expressions and practice by repeating - then you will get the hang of it in no time!

All right! Below are some of the most common expressions in Korean. Knowing these in advance will get you way ahead of others, and help you easily and quickly identify what someone's talking about. Listen and practice.

얼마	ŏl-ma	how much
언제	ŏn-je	when
어디	ŏ-di	where
누가	nu-ga	who
어떻게	ŏ-ttŏ-ke	how
왜	wae	why
~입니다.	~ ip-ni-da.	It's ~
~입니까?	~ ip-ni-gga?	Is it ~ ?
~있습니다.	~ it-ssŭp-ni-da.	There is ~ / I have ~
~없습니다.	~ ŏp-ssŭp-ni-da.	There isn't ~ / I don't have ~
~있습니까?	~ it-ssŭp-ni-gga?	Is there? / Do you have ~ ?
~없습니까?	~ ŏp-ssŭp-ni-gga?	Isn't there ~ ? / Don't you have ~ ?
~할 수 있습니다. / 없습니다.	~ hal su it-ssŭp-ni-da. ~ hal su ŏp-ssŭp-ni-da.	(Subject) can ~ (Subject) can't ~
~할 수 있습니까? /없습니까?	~ hal su it-ssŭp-ni-kka? ~ hal su ŏp-ssŭp-ni-ka?	Can (subject) ~ ? Can't (subject) ~ ?
~해 주세요.	~ hae ju-se-yo.	Please do ~ .
~부탁합니다.	~ bu-tak-hap-ni-da.	~ please.
~어때요?	~ ŏ-ttae-yo?	how is / how about ~ ?
뭐예요?	mwŏ-ye-yo?	what is ~ ?
~싶었습니다.	~ ship-ŏt-ssŭp-ni-da.	has/have been wanting to ~
~하세요.	~ ha-se-yo.	please do ~
~해도 되나요?	~hae-do doe-na-yo?	Is it okay to ~ ?

Well done! You've come a long way - now you are almost ready to learn to make expressions in Korean! Before we finally let you fly on your own, we'd like to show you how to use the book. Please see the description below.

02 만나서 반갑습니다.
man-na-sŏ ban-gap-sŭp-ni-da.

It's nice to meet you.

We've applied different guide marks to separate the parts of a sentence, so you can clearly see which portion corresponds with which, instead of blindly trying to remember a sentence as a whole, because it's a lot more efficient that way. The more parts you know, the more methods you know to create a sentence!

31 많이 보고 싶었어요.
man-i bo-go ship-ŏ-ssŏ-yo.

(Lit) I wanted to see you a lot.

= I've missed you a lot.

Often times, an expression in one language can't be translated directly to another, because of many factors such as a cultural difference, and thus requires a certain degree of liberty in translation. In such cases, we've also included what it literally means in Korean, so you know how an expression has come about and what it means in English as well.

11 실물이 더 멋지네요!
shil-mul i dŏ mŏt-ji-ne-yo!

(Lit) You are more cool in person!

= You look better in person

Remember the little elements called the topic markers, subject markers, and object markers? While there is no English translation for those, we've lightened it in color so you can identify and familiarize yourself with their usage.

08 좋은 말씀 많이 들었습니다.
jo-ŭn mal-ssŭm man-i dŭl-ŏt-sŭp-ni-da.

I've heard many good things (about you).

Lastly, in Korean, some words are implied but not spoken. While it totally makes sense in Korean, you might find it confusing, because it is just not there in the Korean counterpart. Don't worry - whenever this happens, we made it clear by putting what's implied in parenthesis, so you won't miss a thing.

And a few words on Korean honorifics...!

It's well known that the Korean language has a complex honorifics system which reflects the speaker's relationship to the audience. While there are many variants in determining what/when/where/how it's used, the book mainly uses the formal form, because it's the safest bet (no one would frown on you for being too polite). Below are a few examples.

Informal	Polite	Formal
얼마야? ŏl-ma-ya?	얼마예요? ŏl-ma-ye-yo?	얼마입니까? ŏl-ma-ip-ni-gga?
How much is it?		
공부 했어? gong-bu-hae-ssŏ?	공부 했어요? gong-bu-hae-ssŏ-yo?	공부 하셨습니까? gong-bu-ha-shŏt-sŭp-ni-gga?
Did you study?		
의자야. ŭi-ja-ya.	의자예요. ŭi-ja-ye-yo.	의자입니다. ŭi-ja-ip-ni-da.
It's a chair.		
먹었다. mŏg-ŏt-da.	먹었어요. mŏg-ŏ-ssŏ-yo.	먹었습니다. mŏ-gŏ-ssŭp-ni-da.
I ate.		

While the chart above is y no means a complete list of all the Korean honorifics, you can see a pattern.

• For questions, add ~야/어? at the end for informal, ~예요/어요? for polite, and ~ㅂ니까? for formal.

• For normal, add ~야/다 at the end for informal, ~예요/어요 for polite, and ~ㅂ니다 for formal.

 For audio files, please visit :

newampersand.com/SPEAKKOREAN

Chapter 1. Greetings

Listen, repeat, and learn!

Every chapter has a separate audio track for you to study with!

We will say each sentence for a total of four times - slowly twice and at normal speed twice, so you can learn how each portion sounds separately and also as a whole. Read along while you speak and you would have mastered so much of Korean expressions in no time!

Chapter 1. GREETINGS

01 안녕하세요?
an-nyŏng ha-se-yo?

(Lit) Are you at peace? = How are you doing?

02 만나서 반갑습니다.
man-na-sŏ ban-gap-sŭp-ni-da.

It's nice to meet you.

03 저도 반갑습니다.
jŏ-do ban-gap-sŭp-ni-da.

I'm glad, (to meet you) too.

04 처음 뵙겠습니다.
chŏ-ŭm boep-get-sŭp-ni-da.

(Lit) I'm seeing you (for the) first time.

= How do you do?

05 우리 초면이죠?
u-ri cho-myŏn i-jyo?

(Lit) It's our first time seeing, right?

= We've never met before, right?

06 어디서 뵌 것 같아요.
ŏ-di-sŏ boen gŏt gat-a-yo.

(Lit) I think I've seen you somewhere.

= You look familiar.

07 만나뵙고 싶었습니다.
man-na-boep-go ship-ŏt-sŭp-ni-da.

I've been wanting to meet you.

08 오래전부터 만나뵙고 싶었습니다.
o-rae-jŏn-bu-tŏ man-na-boep-go ship-ŏt-sŭp-ni-da.

I've been wanting to meet you for a long time.

09 잘 부탁드립니다.
jal bu-tak-dŭ-rip-ni-da.

I look forward to your kind cooperation.
= I look forward to working with you.

10 좋은 말씀 많이 들었습니다.
jo-ŭn mal-ssŭm man-i dŭl-ŏt-sŭp-ni-da.

I've heard many great sayings (= things) (about you).

11 실물이 더 멋지네요!
shil-mul i dŏ mŏt-ji-ne-yo!
*~ 네요 is used to show one's impressed.

(Lit) You are more cool in person!

= You look better in person

12 과찬입니다.
gwa-chan ip-ni-da.

(Lit) That's an excessive compliment.

= I'm flattered.

13 만나서 영광입니다.
man-na-sŏ yŏng-gwang ip-ni-da.

It's an honor to meet you.

14 저야말로요.
jŏ ya-mal-lo-yo.

(Lit) It's ME (who s honored to meet you).

= Pleasure is all mine.

15 드디어 만났군요!
dŭ-di-ŏ man-nat-gun-nyo!

We've finally met!

16 연락 주셔서 감사합니다.
yŏl-lak ju-shŏ-sŏ gam-sa-hap-ni-da.

Thank you for contacting me.

17 혹시 김철수씨 아니세요?
hok-shi kim-chŏl-su-ssi a-ni-se-yo?
*ssi = "Mr./Ms." Comes after a name.

Aren't you Mr. Kim Cheol-su by any chance?

18 이게 얼마만이죠?
i-ge ŏl-ma-man-i-jyo?

(Lit) How long has this been?
= How long has it been?

19 이게 도대체 누구예요?
i-ge do-de-che nu-gu-ye-yo?

Who in the world is this?

20 저 기억하세요?
jŏ gi-ŏk-ha-se-yo?

Do you remember me?

21 많이 변했죠?
man-i byŏn-haet-jyo?

I've changed a lot, right?

22 전혀요. 예전 그대로네요!
jŏn-hyŏ-yo. ye-jŏn gŭ-dae-ro-ne-yo!

Not at all! It's (= you're) the same as before!

23 말도안돼요!
mal do an-doe-yo!

That doesn't even make sense!

24 정말 많이 변했네요!
jŏng-mal man-i byŏn-haet-ne-yo!

You've really changed a lot!

25 알아보지 못했죠?
al-a-bo-ji mot-haet-jyo?

You couldn't recognize me, right?

26 더 예뻐졌어요.
dŏ ye-bbŏ-jyŏ-ssŏ-yo.

(Lit) You've become more pretty (= prettier).

27 더 멋있어졌어요.
dŏ mŏ-shi-ssŏ-jyŏ-ssŏ-yo.

You've become more fabulous.

28 요즘 다이어트 하고 있어요.
yo-zŭm da-i-ŏ-tŭ ha-go-i-sso-yo.

I've been on a diet recently.

29 그동안 어떻게 지냈어요?
gŭ-dong-an ŏ-ttŏ-ke ji-nae-ssŏ-yo?

How have you been (so far)?

30 잘 지냈어요.
jal ji-nae-ssŏ-yo.

I've been well.

31 많이 보고 싶었어요.
man-i bo-go ship-ŏ-ssŏ-yo.

(Lit) I've wanted to see you a lot.

= I've missed you a lot.

32 당신 생각 많이 했어요.
dang-shin saeng-gak man-i hae-ssŏ-yo.

I've thought about you a lot.

33 정말 오랜만이에요.
jŏng-mal o-raen-man-i-e-yo.

It's really been a long time!

34 앞으로 더 자주 봐요.
ap-ŭ-ro dŏ ja-ju bwa-yo.

We should see more often from now on.

35 좋은 아침!
jo-ŭn a-chim!

Good morning!

16

36 안녕히 주무셨어요?
an-nyŏng-hi ju-mu-shŏ-ssŏ-yo?

(Lit) Did you sleep peacefully?

= Did you sleep well?

37 잘 잤어요. 미나씨는요?
jal ja-ssŏ-yo. mi-na-ssi-nŭn-yo?

I slept well. What about you, (Ms.) Mina?

38 저도 잘 잤어요.
jŏ-do jal ja-ssŏ-yo.

I slept well, too.

39 식사 하셨어요?
shik-sa ha-shŏ-ssŏ-yo?

Have you had a meal?

40 아니요. 아침/점심/저녁 먹었어요?
a-ni-yo. a-chim/jŏm-shim/jŏ-nyŏk mŏg-ŏ-ssŏ-yo?

No. Did you eat breakfast/lunch/dinner?

41 저는 방금 먹었어요.
jŏ nŭn bang-gŭm mŏg-ŏ-ssŏ-yo.

I ate just now.

42 부모님도 건강하시죠?
bu-mo-nim do gŏn-gang ha-shi-jyo?

(Your) parents are healthy (= doing well), too?

43 덕분에요.
dŏk-bun-e-yo.

Thanks to you.

44 건강은 어때요?
gŏn-gang ŭn ŏ-tte-yo?

(Lit) How's (your) health?
= How are you feeling?

45 너무 피곤해요.
nŏ-mu pi-gon-hae-yo.

I'm too tired.

46 많이 바쁘세요?
man-i ba-bbŭ-se-yo?

Are you very busy?

47 숙제가/업무가 많아요.
suk-je ga / ŏp-mu ga man-a-yo.

There is a lot of homework/work.

= I'm up to my neck with homework/work.

48 무리하지 마세요.
mu-ri-ha-ji ma-se-yo.

Don't work too hard.

49 건강이 최고예요.
gŏn-gang i choe-go-ye-yo.

(Lit) Health is best. = Health comes first.

50 맞아요. 그럴게요.
ma-ja-yo. gŭ-rŏl-gge-yo.

You're right. I will.

51 안녕히 계세요.
an-nyŏng-hi gye-se-yo.

(Lit) Stay peacefully.

= Take care. / Good-bye. / So long.

52 안녕히 가세요.
an-nyŏng-hi ga-se-yo.

(Lit) Go/Leave peacefully.

= Take care. / Good-bye. / So long.

53 다음에 또 만나요.
da-ŭm-e tto man-na-yo.

Meet (= see) you again next time.

54 문자 할게요.
mun-ja hal-gge-yo.

I'll text (you).

55 오늘 즐거웠습니다.
o-nŭl jŭl-gŏ-wŏt-sŭp-ni-da.

It was fun today.

56 그때까지 잘 지내세요.
gŭ-ttae gga-ji jal ji-nae-se-yo.

(Lit) Stay well until then.

= Take care until then.

57 건강히 지내세요!
gŏn-gang-hi ji-nae-se-yo!

Stay healthy!

58 연락합시다!
yŏl-lak hap-shi-da!

Let's keep in touch!

Chapter 2. INTRODUCING YOURSELF

01
제 이름은 김철수입니다.
je i-rŭm ŭn kim-chŏl-su ip-ni-da.

My name is Kim Cheol-soo.

02
성함이 어떻게 되세요?
sŏng-ham i ŏ-ttŏ-ke doe-se-yo?

What is (your) name?

03
저는 미나라고 합니다.
jŏ nŭn mi-na ra-go hap-ni-da.

(Lit) I call myself Mina = My name s Mina.

04
제 명함입니다.
je myŏng-ham ip-ni-da.

(This) is my business card.

05
저는 명함이 없어요.
jŏ nŭn myŏng-ham i ŏp-ssŏ-yo.

I don't have a business card.

06
괜찮아요.
gwen-chan-a-yo.

That's fine.

07
대신, 제 전화번호를 드릴게요.
dae-shin, je jŏn-hwa-bŏn-ho rŭl dŭ-ril-gge-yo.

Instead, I will give you my phone number.

08
여기 있습니다.
yŏ-gi it-ssŭp-ni-da.

Here it is.

09
감사합니다.
gam-sa-hap-ni-da

I appreciate it. = Thank you.

10 제 번호 아세요?
je bŏn-ho a-se-yo?

Do you know my number?

11 아니요, 몰라요. / 네, 알아요.
a-ni-yo, mol-la-yo. / ne, al-a-yo.

No, I don't know. / Yes, I do know.

12 이게 제 번호예요.
i-ge je bŏn-ho ye-yo.

This is my number.

13 저장 할게요. / 저장 했어요.
jŏ-jang hal-gge-yo. / jŏ-jang hae-ssŏ-yo.

I will save (it). / I did save (it).

14 이 번호가 맞나요?
i bŏn-ho ga mat-na-yo?

Is this the correct number?

15 네, 맞아요. / 아니요, 틀렸어요.
ne, ma-ja-yo. / a-ni-yo, tŭl-lyŏ-ssŏ-yo.

Yes, it is. / No it isn't.

16 다시 한번 말해주세요.
da-shi han-bŏn mal-hae-ju-se-yo.

Could you please tell me again one more time?

17 직업이 뭐예요?
jig-ŏb i mwŏ-ye-yo?

What is (your) occupation?

18 무엇을 하시나요?
mu-ŏ sŭl ha-shi-na-yo?

What do you do?

19 어떤 일을 하세요?
ŏ-ttŏn il ŭl ha-se-yo?

What kind of work do you do?

= What line of work are you in?

20 회사원 입니다.
hoe-sa-won ip-ni-da.

(Lit) I'm a company employee.
= I work for a company.

21 삼성에 다녀요.
sam-sŏng e da-nyŏ-yo.

(Lit) I go to Samsung. = I work at Samsung.

22 아르바이트를 합니다.
a-rŭ-ba-i-tŭ rŭl hap-ni-da.

I do (= work) part-time.

23 취직 준비 하고 있어요.
chwi-jik jun-bi ha-go i-ssŏ-yo.

(Lit) I'm preparing to get a job.

= I'm in between jobs.

24 저는 학생입니다.
jŏ nŭn hak-saeng ip-ni-da.

I am a student.

25 저도 학생이에요.
jŏ do hak-saeng i-e-yo.

I am a student, too.

26 한국대학교에 다녀요.
han-guk dae-hak-gyo e da-nyŏ-yo.

I go to Hanguk University.

27 어느 학교에 다니세요?
ŏ-nŭ hak-gyo e da-ni-se-yo?

(Lit) Which school do you go to?

= Where do you go to school?

28 저도 거기에서 공부해요.
jŏ do gŏ-gi-e-sŏ gong-bu-hae-yo.

I study there as well.

= I go to the same school as well.

29 전공이 뭐예요?
jŏn-gong i mwŏ-ye-yo?

What's (your) major?

30 어학당에서 한국어를 배우고 있어요.
ŏ-hak-dang e-sŏ han-gug-ŏ rŭl bae-u-go i-ssŏ-yo.

I'm learning Korean (language) at a language school.

31 저는 미국에서 왔어요.
jŏ nŭn mi-guk e-sŏ wa-ssŏ-yo.

I came from the USA.

= I'm from the USA.

32 원래는 일본에서 태어났어요.
wol-lae nŭn il-bon e-sŏ tae-ŏ-na-ssŏ-yo.

I was originally born in Japan.

33 여기가 제 고향이에요.
yŏ-gi ga je go-hyang i-e-yo.

Here is (= This is) my hometown.

34 이제는 여기가 더 편해요.
i-je nŭn yŏ-gi ga dŏ pyŏn-hae-yo.

(Lit) It's more comfortable here now.

I feel more comfortable here now.

35 한국어가 더 편해요.
han-gug-ŏ ga dŏ pyŏn-hae-yo.

(Lit) Korean is more comfortable.

= I'm more comfortable (speaking) Korean.

36 아직 영어가 더 편해요.
a-jik yŏng-ŏ ga dŏ pyŏn-hae-yo.

I'm still more comfortable (speaking) English.

37 어디에서 오셨어요?
ŏ-di e-sŏ o-shŏ-ssŏ-yo?

Where did you come from?

= Where are you from?

38 어느 나라 사람이에요?
ŏ-nŭ na-ra sa-ram i-e-yo?

(Lit) What country are you a person (of)?

= What's your nationality?

39 고향이 어디에요?
go-hyang i ŏ-di-e-yo?

(Lit) Where's (your) hometown?

= Where do you come from (originally)?

40 부산에서 자랐어요.
busan e-sŏ ja-ra-ssŏ-yo.

I was raised in Busan.

41 한국어 잘 못해요.
han-gug-ŏ jal mot-hae-yo.

I can't do (= speak) Korean well.

42 한국어 열심히 공부하고 있어요.
han-gug-ŏ yŏl-shim-hi gong-bu ha-go i-ssŏ-yo.

I'm studying Korean hard.

43 교환학생인가요?
gyo-hwan-hak-saeng in-ga-yo?

Are you an exchange student?

44 아니요, 유학생이에요.
a-ni-yo, yu-hak-saeng i-e-yo.

No, I'm an international student.

= No, I'm studying abroad.

45 한국에는 처음인가요?
han-gug e nŭn chŏ-ŭm in-ga-yo?

Is it (your) first time in Korea?

46 아니요, 한 번 여행 왔었어요.
a-ni-yo, han bŏn yŏ-haeng wa-ssŏ-ssŏ-yo.

No, (I) came on a trip once.

47 그래요? 언제요?
gŭ-rae-yo? ŏn-je-yo?

Is that right? When?

48 삼년 전에 부모님과요.
sam nyŏn jŏn-e bu-mo-nim-gwa-yo.

Three years ago, with (my) parents.

49 하지만 시간이 많이 없었어요.
ha-ji-man shi-gan i man-i ŏp-ssŏ-ssŏ-yo.

But we didn't have much time.

50 좋은 시간 보냈어요?
jo-ŭn shi-gan bo-nae-ssŏ-yo?

Did you spend (= have) a good time?

51 네. 쇼핑을 너무 많이 했어요.
ne. sho-ping ŭl nŏ-mu man-i hae-ssŏ-yo.

Yes. (We) did too much shopping.

52 부모님은 미국에 계세요.
bu-mo-nim ŭn mi-guk e gye-se-yo.

(My) parents are in the USA.

53 형제가 셋 있어요.
hyŏng-je ga set i-ssŏ-yo.

I have three siblings.

54 제가 가장 어려요.
je ga ga-jang ŏ-ryŏ-yo.

I am most (= the) youngest.

55 제가 가장 나이가 많아요.
je ga ga-jang na-i ga man-a-yo.

(Lit) I have the most age. = I'm the oldest.

56 한국 드라마를 많이 봤어요.
han-gug dŭ-ra-ma rŭl man-i bwa-ssŏ-yo.

I watched a lot of Korean dramas.

57 한국 친구들이 많이 있었어요.
han-gug chin-gu-dŭl i man-i i-ssŏ-ssŏ-yo.

I had many Koren friends.

58 한국 사람 좋아해요.
han-gug sa-ram jo-a-hae-yo.

I like Korean people.

59 한국 음식은 맛있어요.
han-gug ŭm-shig ŭn ma-shi-ssŏ-yo.

Korean food is tasty/delicious.

60 저는 스물 셋 입니다.
jŏ nŭn sŭ-mul set ip-ni-da.

I am twenty-three.

61 실례지만, 나이가 어떻게 되세요?
shil-lye-ji-man, na-i-ga ŏ-ttŏ-ke doe-se-yo?

(Lit) Pardon me, but what is (your) age?

= May I ask how old you are?

62 어디에 사세요?
ŏ-di e sa-se-yo?

(At) where do you live?

63 기숙사에 살아요.
gi-suk-sa e sal-a-yo.

I live in a dorm.

64 곧 이사 할거예요.
got i-sa hal-gŏ-ye-yo.

I will move soon.

65 취미는 뭐예요?
chwi-mi nŭn mwŏ-ye-yo?

(Lit) What's (your) hobby?
= What do you enjoy doing?
/ Do you have any hobbies?

66 음악 듣는 것을 좋아해요.
ŭm-ak dŭt-nŭn gŏ sŭl jo-a-hae-yo.

I like listening to music.

67 어떤 음악이요?
ŏ-ttŏn ŭm-ag i-yo?

What kind of music (is it)?

68 뭐든지 상관 안해요.
mwŏ-dŭn-ji sang-gwan an-hae-yo.

I don't care whatever it is.

69 당신은요?
dang-shin ŭn yo?

(And) you?

70 영화 보는 것이 가장 좋아요.
yŏng-hwa bo-nŭn gŏ shi ga-jang jo-a-yo.

I like watching movies the most.

71 우리 언제 영화 보러 가요!
u-ri ŏn-je yŏng-hwa bo-rŏ ga-yo!

We should go (to) watch a movie sometime!

Chapter 3. AT SCHOOL

01 여기 학생인가요?
yŏ-gi hak-saeng in-ga-yo?

Are you a student here?

02 학생증을 보여주세요.
hak-saeng-tzŭng ŭl bo-yŏ-ju-se-yo.

Show me (your) student I.D. card, please.

03 학생증을 아직 못 만들었어요.
hak-saeng-tzŭng ŭl a-jik mot man-dŭl-ŏ-ssŏ-yo.

I couldn't make (my) student I.D. card yet.

04 저는 신입생이에요.
jŏ nŭn shin-ip-saeng i-e-yo.

I am a new student.

05 대학원생이에요.
dae-hag-won-saeng i-e-yo.

(I) am a grad student.

06 학부생이에요.
hak-bu-saeng i-e-yo.

(I) am an undergrad student.

07 교실이 어디죠?
gyo-shil i ŏ-di-jyo?

Where is the classroom?

08 수업이 몇시죠?
su-ŏb i myŏ-sshi-jyo?

What time is the class?

09 자리에 앉으세요.
ja-ri e an-zŭ-se-yo.

Please get seated in (your) seat.

10 책을 꺼내세요.
chaeg ŭl ggŏ-nae-se-yo.

Take out (your) book, please.

11 12 페이지를 펴세요.
shib-i pe-i-ji rŭl pyŏ-se-yo.

Open to page 12, please.

12 수업을 시작합시다.
su-ŏb ŭl shi-jak-hap-shi-da.

(Lit) Let's start the lesson.

= Let's get started with the lesson.

13 출석을 부르겠습니다.
chul-sŏg ŭl bu-rŭ-get-ssŭp-ni-da.

I will call the roll.

14 지각입니다.
ji-gag ip-ni-da.

(You are/He is/She is/I am) tardy.

15 결석입니다.
gyŏl-ssŏg ip-ni-da.

(You are/He is/She is/I am) absent.

16 지각해서 죄송합니다.
ji-gak-hae-sŏ joe-song-hap-ni-da.

I am sorry for being tardy.

17 조용히 하세요.
jo-yong-hi ha-se-yo.

Please be quiet.

18 질문있습니다.
jil-mun it-ssŭp-ni-da.

I have a question.

19 잘 이해가 되지 않습니다.
jal i-hae ga doe-ji an-ssŭp-ni-da.

I can't understand well.

20 제가 맞게 이해하고 있나요?
je ga mat-ge i-hae-ha-go it-na-yo?

(Lit) Am I understanding (it) correctly?

= Do I understand it right?

21 잘 보이지 않아요.
jal bo-i-ji an-a-yo.

(Lit) It's not well viewable.

= I can't see it very well.

22 조금 더 크게 말씀해주세요.
jo-gŭm dŏ kŭ-ge mal-ssŭm-hae-ju-se-yo.

(Lit) Please speak a little more loudly.

= Could you please speak up?

23 다시 한번 말씀해주세요.
da-shi han-bŏn mal-ssŭm-hae-ju-se-yo.

Please say it one more time.

24 잘 모르겠어요.
jal mo-rŭ-get-ssŏ-yo.

I don't know (it) well. / I'm not sure.

25 문제가 어렵네요.
mun-je ga ŏ-ryŏp-ne-yo.

(Lit) The question is difficult.
= It's a difficult question.

26 배웠어요?
bae-wŏ-ssŏ-yo.

Have you learned?

27 아직 배우지 못했어요.
a-jik bae-u-ji mot-haet-ssŏ-yo.

(Lit) I couldn't (= haven't) learn(ed) yet.

28 수업은 몇시에 끝나죠?
su-ŏb ŭn myŏ-sshi-e ggŭt-na-jyo?

At what time does the class end?

29 학교식당은 어디죠?
hak-gyo shik-dang ŭn ŏ-di-jyo?

Where is the school cafeteria?

30 점심시간이 언제죠?
jŏm-shim shi-gan i ŏn-je-jyo?

When is lunchtime?

31 점심 같이 먹을까요?
jŏm-shim ga-chi mŏ-gŭl-gga-yo?

Shall we eat (= have) lunch together?

32 숙제 같이 할래요?
suk-je ga-chi hal-lae-yo?

Want to do the homework together?

33 도와주세요.
do-wa-ju-se-yo.

Please help me.

34 외국인이라 잘 몰라요.
oe-gug-in i-ra jal mol-la-yo.

I don't know (it) well because (I'm) a foreigner.

35 기숙사에 어떻게 가죠?
gi-suk-sa e ŏ-tto-ke ga-jyo?

How do you get to the dorm?

36 몇시가 통금인가요?
myŏ-sshi ga tong-gŭm in-ga-yo?

What time is the curfew?

37 숙제를 깜빡했어요.
suk-je rŭl ggam-bbak-hae-ssŏ-yo.

(I) forgot (to do) the homework.

38 제가 착각했나봐요.
je ga chak-gak haet-na-bwa-yo.

I must have gotten confused.

39 성적표 봤어요?
sŏng-jŏk-pyo bwa-ssŏ-yo?

Have you seen (your) report card?

40 성적표 언제 나와요?
sŏng-jŏk-pyo ŏn-je na-wa-yo?

When do the report cards come out?

41 성적이 엉망이에요.
sŏng-jŏg i ŏng-mang i-e-yo.

(My) grades are a mess.

42 이번 학기는 성적이 좋지 않아요.
i-bŏn hak-gi nŭn sŏng-jŏg i jot-chi an-a-yo.

(My) grades aren't good this semester.

43 다음 학기에는 열심히 할거에요.
da-ŭm hak-gi e nŭn yŏl-shim-hi hal-gŏ-e-yo.

I will try hard next semester.

44 적응이 힘들어요.
jŏg-ŭng i him-dŭl-ŏ-yo.

It's difficult getting used to (the new environment).
= I've been feeling out of element.

45 친구들이 많이 있어요/없어요.
chin-gu-dŭl i man-i i-ssŏ-yo / ŏp-ssŏ-yo.

(I) have/don't have many friends.

46 교수님 한번만 봐주세요.
gyo-su-nim han-bŏn-man bwa-ju-se-yo.

Professor, please give me a break just once.

47 이메일 보내드렸어요.
i-mae-il bo-nae-dŭ-ryŏ-ssŏ-yo.

I've sent you an email.

48 수업이 취소되었어요.
su-ŏb i chwi-so-doe-ŏ-ssŏ-yo.

The class has been canceled.

49 이번 학기는 정말 바쁘네요.
i-bŏn hak-gi nŭn jŏng-mal ba-bbŭ-ne-yo.

This semester is really busy.

50 수업을 많이 듣고 있어요.
su-ŏb ŭl man-i dŭt-go i-ssŏ-yo.

(I) am taking many classes.

51 아르바이트도 할 수 있나요?
a-rŭ-ba-i-tŭ do hal-su-it-na-yo?

Can I also work part-time?

52 학비가 너무 비싸요!
hak-bi ga nŏ-mu bi-ssa-yo!

Tuition is too expensive!

53 장학금을 신청하고 싶어요.
jang-hak-gŭm ŭl shin-chŏng ha-go ship-ŏ-yo.

I'd like to apply for a scholarship.

54 경비원에게 물어보세요.
gyŏng-bi-won e-ge mul-ŏ-bo-se-yo.

Ask (to) the security, please.

55 캠퍼스가 너무 넓어요.
kaem-pŏ-sŭ ga nŏ-mu nŏl-bŏ-yo.

The campus is too vast/wide.

56 도서관은 어디죠?
do-sŏ-gwan ŭn ŏ-di-jyo?

Where is the library?

57 도서관에서 공부 합니다.
do-sŏ-gwan e-sŏ gong-bu hap-ni-da.

(I) study at the library.

58 사람이 정말 많네요!
sa-ram i jŏng-mal man-ne-yo!

There are really a lot of people!

59 여기에서 공부 해도 되나요?
yŏ-gi e-sŏ gong-bu hae-do doe-na-yo?

May I study (at) here?

60 동아리에 가입하고 싶어요.
dong-a-ri e ga-ip ha-go ship-ŏ-yo.

I'd like to join (to) a club.

61 어떤 동아리가 있나요?
ŏ-ttŏn dong-a-ri ga it-na-yo?

What kind of clubs are there?

62 전공을 아직 못정했어요.
jŏn-gong ŭl a-jik mot-jŏng-hae-ssŏ-yo.

(I) couldn't decide (my) major yet.

= I haven't declared my major yet.

63 제 전공은 미술입니다.
je jŏn-gong ŭn mi-sul ip-ni-da.

My major is art. = I major in art.

64 어려운 과목이에요.
ŏ-ryŏ-un gwa-mog i-e-yo.

It's a difficult subject.

65 깜빡 졸았네요.
ggam-bbak jol-at-ne-yo.

I fell into a doze.

66 깨워주세요.
ggae-wŏ ju-se-yo.

Wake me up, please.

67 필기 했어요?
pil-gi hae-ssŏ-yo?

Did you take notes?

68 노트좀 빌려주세요.
no-tŭ jom bil-lyŏ-ju-se-yo.

Let me borrow (your) notebook a little, please.

69 책 좀 같이 봐도 될까요?
chaek jom ga-chi bwa-do doel-gga-yo?

(Lit) May I look at (= share) the book a little together (= with you)?

70 이게 무슨 뜻이죠?
i-ge mu-sŭn ttŭ-shi-jyo?

What is the meaning of this?

= What does this mean?

71 영어로는 뭐라고 하죠?
yŏng-ŏ-ro nŭn mwŏ-ra-go ha-jyo?

How do you say (it) in English?

72 교수님께 여쭤 보세요.
gyo-su-nim-gge yŏ-jjwŏ bo-se-yo.

Ask (to) the professor.

73 교수실에 계세요?
gyo-su-shil e gye-se-yo?

Are you in the Professor's office?

74 언제 찾아뵈면 좋을까요?
ŏn-je cha-ja-boe-myŏn jo-ŭl-gga-yo?

When would be (a) good (time) to visit you?

75 열심히 공부할게요.
yŏl-shim-hi gong-bu hal-e-yo.

I will study hard.

76 혹시 김하나 교수님 아세요?
hok-shi kim-ha-na gyo-su-nim a-se-yo?

Do you know Professor Kim Ha-na, by any chance?

77 정말 좋은 분이에요.
jŏng-mal jo-ŭn buni-e-yo.

(She/He) is a really nice person.

78 알아요. 저 예전에 수업 들었어요.
al-a-yo. jǒ ye-jǒn-e su-ǒp dǔl-ǒ-ssǒ-yo.

I do know. I took (her) class in the past.

79 수업은 어떤가요?
su-ǒb ǔn ǒ-ttǒn-ga-yo?

How is (the) class?

80 쉬운가요? / 어려운가요?
shwi-un-ga-yo? ǒ-ryǒ-un-ga-yo?

Is it easy? / Difficult?

81 정말 쉬워요. / 어려워요.
jǒng-mal shwi-wǒ-yo / ǒ-ryǒ-wǒ-yo.

It's really easy. / difficult.

82 수업이 재미있나요?
su-ǒb i jae-mi-it-na-yo?

Is the class fun?

83 과제가 많나요?
gwa-je ga man-na-yo?

Are there a lot of assignments?

= Does he/she assign a lot of assignments?

84 그룹 프로젝트가 많아요.
gǔ-rǔp pǔ-ro-jek-tǔ ga man-a-yo.

There are a lot of group projects.

85 시험을 자주 보나요?
shi-hǒm ǔl ja-ju bo-na-yo?

Do (you) take tests often?

= Does he/she test you often?

86 신입생 환영회가 있어요.
shin-ip-saeng hwan-yǒng-hoe ga i-ssǒ-yo.

There is a welcome party for the freshmen.

87 선배님, 안녕하세요!
sǒn-bae-nim, an-nyǒng-ha-se-yo!

How are you, sunbaenim!

*sunbaenim = one's senior at school, or
someone who joined an organization earlier

88 동아리 가입을 환영합니다.
dong-a-ri ga-ib ǔl hwan-yǒng-hap-ni-da.

We welcome you for joining the club!

89 열심히 참여하세요.
yǒl-shim-hi cham-yǒ ha-se-yo.

(Lit) Participate actively.

We look forward to your active participation.

90 빠지지 말고 나오세요.
bba-ji-ji mal-go na-o-se-yo.

Please attend without skipping.

91 도움이 필요하면 말하세요.
do-um i pil-yo-ha-myǒn mal-ha-se-yo.

Tell me if you need help.

31

Chapter 4. SHOPPING

01 어서오세요.
ŏ-sŏ-o-se-yo.
Welcome.

02 무엇을 찾으시나요?
mu-ŏ sŭl cha-zŭ-shi-na-yo?
What are you looking for?

03 혹시 반바지 있나요?
hok-shi ban-ba-ji it-na-yo?
Do you have shorts by any chance?

04 모자를/신발을 찾고 있어요.
mo-ja rŭl / shin-bal ŭl chat-go i-ssŏ-yo.
I'm looking for hats/shoes.

05 찾으시는 스타일이/브랜드가 있나요?
cha-zŭ-shi-nŭn sŭ-ta-il i / bŭ-raen-dŭ ga it-na-yo?
Is there a style/brand you are looking for?

06 도와드릴까요?
do-wa-dŭ-ril-gga-yo?
May I help you?

07 사이즈가 어떻게 되시나요?
sa-i-zŭ ga ŏ-ttŏ-ke doe-shi-na-yo?
What is (your) size?

08 입어봐도 되나요?
ib-ŏ-bwa-do doe-na-yo?
Can I try (this) on?

09 이 사이즈 있나요?
i sa-i-zŭ it-na-yo?
Do you have this size?

10 제 사이즈는 30입니다.
je sa-i-zŭ nŭn sam-ship ip-ni-da.

My size is 30. = I'm a 30.

11 조금 큰/작은 것 같아요.
jo-gŭm kŭn / jag-ŭn gŏt gat-a-yo.

I think it's a little small/big.

12 딱 맞네요.
ttak mat-ne-yo.

It fits perfectly.

13 얼마예요?
ŏl-ma ye-yo?

How much is it?

14 세일 하나요?
se-il ha-na-yo?

Is it on sale?

15 재고 있나요?
jae-go it-na-yo?

Do you have (it) in stock?

16 확인해 주시겠어요?
hwag-in hae ju-shi-get-ssŏ-yo?

Could you check, please?

17 반품 가능한가요?
ban-pum ga-nŭng-han-ga-yo?

Is it possible to return? = Is it returnable?

18 얼마동안에 반품 할 수 있나요?
ŏl-ma dong-an-e ban-pum hal su it-na-yo?

(Lit) Within how long can I return?

= How late can I return it?

19 환불 가능한가요?
hwan-bul ga-nŭng-han-ga-yo?

(Lit) Is a refund possible?

= Can I get a refund?

20 반품 하고 싶습니다.
ban-pum ha-go ship-sŭp-ni-da.

I'd like to return.

21 제품에 문제가 있나요?
je-pum e mun-je ga it-na-yo?

Was there a problem with the product?

22 아니요, 사이즈가 맞지 않아요.
a-ni-yo, sa-i-zŭ ga mat-ji an-a-yo.

(Lit) No, the size isn't right.

= No, it doesn't fit.

23 아니요, 스타일이 맞지 않아요.
a-ni-yo, sŭ-ta-il i mat-ji a-na-yo.

(Lit) No, the style isn't right.

= No, I didn't like the style.

24 다른 색상이 있나요?
da-rŭn saek-sang i it-na-yo?

Do you have different colors?

25 이게 마음에 들어요.
i-ge ma-ŭm-e dŭl-ŏ-yo.

(Lit) This is to (my) liking. = I like this.

26 그냥 둘러볼게요.
gŭ-nyang dul-lŏ-bol-gge-yo.

I'll just look around.

27 구경해도 되나요?
gu-gyŏng-hae-do doe-na-yo?

May I look around?

28 탈의실이 어디죠?
tal-ŭi-shil i ŏ-di-jyo?

Where is the fitting room?

29 남성용/여성용 인가요?
nam-sŏng-yong / yŏ-sŏng-yong in-ga-yo?

Is (this) for men/for women?

= Is this men's or women's?

30 여기 흠이 있어요.
yŏ-gi hŭm i i-ssŏ-yo.

There is a scratch/nick/defect here.

31 원래 이런가요?
wŏl-lae i-rŏn-ga-yo?

Is this usually like this? = Is this normal?

32 할인 해 주실수 있나요?
hal-in hae ju-shil-su it-na-yo?

(Lit) Can you discount it for me?

= Can you give me a discount?

33 신상품 있나요?
shin-sang-pum it-na-yo?

Do you have the latest products?

34 정품 맞나요?
jŏng-pum mat-na-yo?

Is this an authentic product?

35 매니저를 만나고 싶습니다.
mae-ni-jŏ rŭl man-na-go ship-sŭp-ni-da.

I'd like to meet the manager.

34

36 계산 해주세요.
gye-san hae-ju-se-yo.

(Lit) Please calculate (it) for me.

Please ring it up for me.

37 쇼핑백을 주세요.
sho-ping-baeg ŭl ju-se-yo.

Please give me a shopping bag.

38 포장 해주세요.
po-jang hae-ju-se-yo.

(Lit) Please wrap (it) for me.

= I'd like to have it wrapped.

39 영수증을 백안에 넣어주세요.
yŏng-su-zŭng ŭl baeg-an-e nŏ-ŏ-ju-se-yo.

Please put the receipt in the bag.

40 영수증은 저에게 주세요.
yŏng-su-zŭng ŭn jŏ-e-ge ju-se-yo.

Please give the receipt to me.

41 카드 되나요?
ka-dŭ doe-na-yo?

Is (a credit) card okay?

= Do you take credit cards?

42 현금도 되나요?
hyŏn-gŭm do doe-na-yo?

Is cash okay, too? = Can I pay with cash?

43 현금으로 사면 할인 받나요?
hyŏn-gŭm ŭ-ro sa-myŏn hal-in bat-na-yo?

Do I receive a discount if I buy with cash?

44 택스리펀드 되나요?
taek-sŭ-ri-pŏn-dŭ doe-na-yo?

Is it eligible for a tax refund?

45 택스리펀드는 어디에서 하나요?
taek-sŭ-ri-pŏn-dŭ nŭn ŏ-di-e-sŏ ha-na-yo?

(From) where do I do (= file) tax refund?

46 이렇게 작성하면 되나요?
i-rŏt-ke jak-sŏng-ha-myŏn doe-na-yo?

(Lit) Is it right if I fill (it) out like this?

47 배달도 되나요?
bae-dal do doe-na-yo?

Can it be delivered as well?

48 홀드해 주실 수 있나요?
hol-dŭ hae ju-shil su it-na-yo?

Can you hold (it) for me?

49 다시 찾으러 올게요.
da-shi cha-zŭ-rŏ ol-gge-yo.

I'll come again to pick it up.

50 수선 가능한가요?
su-sŏn ga-nŭng-han-ga-yo?

Is alternation possible?

51 언제 준비 될까요?
ŏn-je jun-bi doel-gga-yo?

When will it be ready?

52 준비되면 연락 주세요.
jun-bi doe-myŏn yŏl-lak ju-se-yo.

Please give me a call if (= when) it's ready.

53 도와주셔서 감사합니다.
do-wa-ju-shŏ-sŏ gam-sa-hap-ni-da.

Thanks for helping me. = Thanks for your help.

54 그때 돌아 올게요.
gŭ-ttae dol-a-ol-gge-yo.

I'll be back then.

55 좀 더 깎아주세요.
jom dŏ gga-ka-ju-se-yo.

Please give me a little more discount.

56 너무 비싸네요.
nŏ-mu bi-ssa-ne-yo.

It's too expensive.

57 좀 더 싼 거 있나요?
jom dŏ ssan gŏ it-na-yo?

Do you have anything a little more cheap (= cheaper)?

58 영업시간이 어떻게 되요?
yŏng-ŏp-shi-gan i ŏ-ttŏ-ke doe-yo?

What are (your) business hours?

59 몇시에 열어요?
myŏ-sshi e yŏl-ŏ-yo?

(At) what time do (you) open?

60 몇시에 닫아요?
myŏ-sshi e dad-a-yo?

(At) what time do (you) close?

61 오늘 몇시까지 하세요?
o-nŭl myŏ-sshi gga-ji ha-se-yo?

(Lit) Until what time do you work today?

= How late do you open today?

62 어떻게 계산하시겠어요?
ŏ-ttŏ-ke gye-san ha-shi-get-ssŏ-yo?

How would you like to pay?

63 더 가져 올게요.
dŏ ga-jyŏ ol-gge-yo.

I will bring more.

36

64 잠시만 기다려주세요.
jam-shi-man gi-da-ryŏ-ju-se-yo.
Please wait a moment.

65 함께 계산 해주세요.
ham-gge gye-san hae-ju-se-yo.
Ring them up together, please.
= I'd like to pay for them all together.

66 따로따로 계산 해주세요.
tta-ro-tta-ro gye-san hae-ju-se-yo.
Ring them up separately, please.
= I'd like to pay for them separately.

67 돈이 모자라네요.
don i mo-ja-ra-ne-yo.
(Lit) Money is insufficient.
= I don't have enough money.

68 얼마나 더 필요하죠?
ŏl-ma-na dŏ pil-yo-ha-jyo?
How much more do you need

69 새 제품 맞죠?
sae je-pum mat-jyo?
It's a new product, right?

70 언제 재입고 될까요?
ŏn-je jae-ip-go doel-gga-yo?
When will it be re-stocked?

71 다른 매장에는 있나요?
da-rŭn mae-jang-e nŭn it-na-yo?
Is it available at other stores?

72 디스플레이랑 같은 것 주세요.
di-sŭ-pŭl-lae-i-lang ga-tŭn gŏt ju-se-yo.
Please give me the same thing as (what's on) display.

73 어떤게 가장 인기있나요?
ŏ-ttŏn-ge ga-jang in-ggi-it-na-yo?
Which is the most popular?

74 재질이 뭔가요?
jae-jil i mwŏn-ga-yo?
What is the material? = What's it made of?

75 늘려주세요/줄여주세요.
nŭl-lyŏ-ju-se-yo / jul-yŏ-ju-se-yo.
Please have it extended/Please have it shortened.

76 세탁기에 돌려도 되나요?
se-tak-gi e dol-lyŏ-do doe-na-yo?
(Lit) Can I spin it in a washer?
= Is it machine washable?

77 교환하고 싶어요.
gyo-hwan ha-go ship-ŏ-yo.
I'd like to exchange (this).

78 이거 보증 되나요?
i-gŏ bo-zŭng doe-na-yo?
Can this be covered by warranty?

79 계산이 잘못 된 것 같아요.
gye-san i jal-mot doen gŏt gat-a-yo.

(Lit) I think the calculation is wrong.

= I think the bill is incorrect.

80 어때보여요?
ŏ-tte bo-yŏ-yo?

How do I look?

81 잘 어울리나요?
jal ŏ-ul-li-na-yo?

Does (it) look good on me?

82 이걸로 할게요.
i-gŏl lo hal-gge-yo.

I'll go with this.

83 지금 유행이에요.
ji-gŭm yu-haeng-i-e-yo.

(This) is in fashion now.

= This is popular these days.

84 추천해 주세요.
chu-chŏn hae ju-se-yo.

Please suggest for me.

= I'm open to suggestions.

85 가격이 어떻게 되나요?
ga-gyŏg i ŏ-ttŏ-ke doe-na-yo?

What's the price?

86 다 고르셨나요?
da go-rŭ-shŏt-na-yo?

(Lit) Have you picked/selected all?

= Did you find everything all right?

87 전부 얼마죠?
jŏn-bu ŏl-ma-jyo?

How much is it all together?

88 세금이 포함되었나요?
se-gŭm i po-ham doe-ŏt-na-yo?

Are taxes included?

89 거스름 돈 있으세요?
gŏ-sŭ-rŭm don i-ssŭ-se-yo?

Do you have change (money)?

90 싸게 사시는 겁니다.
ssa-ge sa-shi-nŭn gŏp-ni-da.

(Lit) You are buying it cheaply.

= This is a good buy.

91 세일은 언제까지 하나요?
se-il ŭn ŏn-je gga-ji ha-na-yo?

(Lit) Until when do you do the sale?

= How long is the sale for?

92 지금은 특별 세일 기간입니다.
ji-gŭm ŭn tŭk-byŏl se-il gi-gan ip-ni-da.

Now (= It) is a special sale period.

93 돈을 더 낸 것 같아요.
don ŭl dŏ naen gŏt gat-a-yo.

I think (I) paid more money.

= I think I overpaid.

94 신용카드를/여행자수표를 받나요?
shin-yong-ka-dŭ rŭl/ yŏ-haeng-ja-su-pyo rŭl bat-na-yo?
Do you take credit card/traveler's checks?

95 엘레베이터는 어디에 있나요?
el-le-be-i-tŏ nŭn ŏ-di-e it-na-yo?
Where is the elevator?

96 이것을 수리받고 싶어요.
i-gŏ sŭl su-ri-bat-go ship-ŏ-yo.
I'd like to have this repaired.

97 고장났어요.
go-jang-na-ssŏ-yo.
It's broken.

98 불량품이에요.
bul-lyang-pum i-e-yo.
It's a defective product.

99 어디서 샀어요?
ŏ-di-sŏ sa-sso-yo?
(From) where did (you) buy (it)?

100 정말 옷 잘입네요.
jŏng-mal ot jal ip-ne-yo.
(Lit) (You) really wear clothes well.
= You have a great sense of fashion.

101 패션 감각이 좋다.
pae-shŏn gam-gag i jot-ta.
(Lit) (Your) sense of fashion is good.

102 옷이 그게 뭐예요?
o shi gŭ-ge mwŏ-ya?
What's with the clothes?

103 요즘 유행하는 스타일이에요.
yo-zŭm yu-haeng-ha-nŭn sŭ-ta-il i-ye-yo.
(This) is a style that's in trend these days.

104 옷이 날개네요.
o shi nal-gae ne-yo.
(Lit) Clothes are wings.
= You look so fine in those clothes.

105 옷이 너무 야해요.
o shi nŏ-mu ya-hae-yo.
(Your) clothes are too sexy/revealing.

Chapter 5. AT THE RESTAURANT

01 자리 있나요?
ja-ri it-na-yo?

Is there a seat (available)?

02 몇 명 이세요?
myŏt myŏng i-se-yo?

How many people is it?

03 네명 입니다.
ne myŏng ip-ni-da.

It's 4 people.

04 예약 하셨나요?
ye-yak ha-shŏt-na-yo?

Did you make a reservation?

= Do you have a reservation?

05 아니요, 안 했어요 / 네, 했어요.
a-ni-yo,   an hae-ssŏ-yo. / ne, hae-ssŏ-yo.

No, I did not. / Yes, I did.

06 몇시로 예약 하셨나요?
myŏ-sshi ro ye-yak ha-shŏt-na-yo?

What time did you make the reservation for?

07 한시요. / 한시 삼십분이요.
han shi-yo. / han shi sam-ship bun i-yo.

It's 1 o'clock. /

(Lit) It's 1 o'clock and thirty minutes.

08 이쪽으로 오세요.
i-jjog ŭ-ro   o-se-yo.

Come (to) this way, please.

09 이 자리 괜찮으세요?
i   ja-ri goen-chan-ŭ-se-yo?

Is this seat okay?

10 혹시 테이블은 없나요?
hok-shi te-i-bŭl ŭn ŏp-na-yo?

Don't you have a table, by any chance?

11 메뉴를 주세요.
me-nyu rŭl ju-se-yo.

Give me the menu, please.

12 추천 해주세요.
chu-chŏn hae-ju-se-yo.

Please make suggestions/recommendations.

13 매운 것/단 것 좋아하세요?
mae-un gŏt/dan gŏt jo-a-ha-se-yo?

Do you like something spicy/
something sweet?

14 매운 것 잘 못먹어요
mae-un gŏt jal mot-mŏg-o-yo.

(I) can't eat spicy things well.

15 이거 드셔보셨나요?
i-gŏ dŭ-shŏ-bo-shŏt-na-yo?

Have you tried this?

16 어떤 요리인가요?
ŏ-ttŏn yo-ri in-ga-yo?

What kind of dish/cuisine is it?

17 마늘이/양파가 들어있나요?
ma-nŭl i / yang-pa ga dŭl-ŏ-it-na-yo?

Does it have garlic/onion in it?

18 뭘로 만든 건가요?
mwŏl-lo man-dŭn gŏn-ga-yo?

(Lit) With what is it made?

19 얼마나 걸리나요?
ŏl-ma-na gŏl-li-na-yo?

How long does it take?

20 시간이 좀 걸립니다
shi-gan i jom gŏl-lip-ni-da.

It will take a little time (to cook).

21 양이 얼마나 되나요?
yang i ŏl-ma-na doe-na-yo?

(Lit) How much is the portion?

22 둘이 먹기에 충분해요/부족해요.
dul i mŏk-ki-e chung-bun-hae-yo / bu-jok-hae-yo.

It's enough (for) two to eat. / It's inadequate.

23 음료수는 어떤 종류로 하시겠어요?
ŭm-nyo-su nŭn ŏ-ttŏn jong-nyu ro ha-shi-get-ssŏ-yo?.

(Lit) What kind of beverage would you like to go with?

24 어떤게 있나요?
ŏ-ttŏn-ge it-na-yo?

What kind of thing (= beverage) do you have?

25 쥬스로 할게요.
jyu-sŭ ro hal-gge-yo.

I'll go with juice.

26 그냥 물이요.
gŭ-nyang mul i-yo.

(Lit) It's just water. = Just water, please.

27 젓가락/포크/숟가락/냅킨 주세요.
jŏt-ga-rak/po-kŭ/sut-ga-rak/naep-kin ju-se-yo.

Please give me chopsticks/a fork/a spoon.

28 주문 하시겠어요?
ju-mun ha-shi-get-ssŏ-yo?

Would you like to order?

29 주문 도와드릴까요?
ju-mun do-wa-dŭ-ril-gga-yo?

May I help you (with your) order?

30 시간을 조금 더 주세요.
shi-gan ŭl jo-gŭm dŏ ju-se-yo.

Give me a little more time, please.

31 주문하신 음식 나왔습니다.
ju-mun-ha-shin ŭm-shik na-wat-ssŭp-ni-da.

(Lit) The dish you ordered came out.

= Here is the dish you ordered.

32 이건 제가 주문한게 아닌데요.
i-gŏn je ga ju-mun-han-ge a-nin-de-yo.

This is not what I ordered.

33 다시 확인 해주세요.
da-shi hwag-in hae-ju-se-yo.

Check again, please.

34 사진과 너무 다른데요.
sa-jin gwa nŏ-mu da-rŭn-de-yo.

It's too different from the picture.

35 주방장을 불러주세요.
ju-bang-jang ŭl bul-lŏ-ju-se-yo.

Bring me the chef, please.

36 음식이 식었어요.
ŭm-shig i shig-ŏ-ssŏ-yo.

(Lit) The food has cooled. = The food is cold.

37 음식에서 이게 나왔어요.
ŭm-shig e-sŏ i-ge na-wa-ssŏ-yo.

(Lit) This came out from the food.

= This was in my food.

38 음식이 너무 짜요/싱거워요.
ŭm-shig i nŏ-mu jja-yo / shing-gŏ-wŏ-yo.

The food is too salty/bland.

39 이건 어떻게 먹나요?
i-gŏn ŏ-ttŏ-ke mŏk-na-yo?

How do you eat this?

40 음식 언제 나오나요?
ŭm-shig ŏn-je na-o-na-yo?

When does the food come out?

41 왜 이렇게 오래 걸리죠?
wae i-rŏt-ke o-rae gŏl-li-jyo?

Why does it take this long?

42 주문이 들어갔나요?
ju-mun i dŭl-ŏ-gat-na-yo?

Did the order go through?

43 계산서를 주세요.
gye-san-sŏ rŭl ju-se-yo.

Please give me the bill.

44 잘 먹었습니다.
jal mŏg-ŏ-ssŭp-ni-da.

(Lit) (I) ate well.

= Thanks for the great meal.

45 정말 맛있었어요.
jŏng-mal ma-shi-ssŏ-ssŏ-yo.

It was really delicious.

46 배가 불러요.
bae ga bul-lŏ-yo

(My) stomach is full. = I'm full.

47 포장 되나요?
po-jang doe-na-yo.

(Lit) Can it be wrapped?

= Can I take this out?

48 남은 음식을 싸주세요.
nam-ŭn ŭm-shig ŭl ssa-ju-se-yo.

(Lit) Please wrap the leftover (meal).

= I'd like a doggy bag, please

Chapter 6. AT THE AIRPORT

01 어느 항공 인가요?
ŏ-nŭ hang-gong in-ga-yo?

Which airline is it?

02 한국항공 입니다.
han-guk hang-gong ip-ni-da.

It's Hanguk Airline.

03 201 항공편 입니다.
i-gong-il hang-gong-pyŏn ip-ni-da.

It's flight 201.

04 여권을 보여주세요.
yŏ-ggwŏn ŭl bo-yŏ-ju-se-yo.

Show me the passport, please.

05 예약을 확인 해주세요.
ye-yag ŭl hwag-in hae-ju-se-yo.

Could you please confirm (my) reservation?

06 이번/다음 터미널에 내려주세요.
i-bŏn / da-ŭm tŏ-mi-nŏl e nae-ryŏ-ju-se-yo.

Please drop me off at this/next terminal.

07 수속을 하려고요.
su-sog ŭl ha-ryŏ-go-yo.

I'd like to check in, please.

08 수속 카운터는 어디인가요?
su-sok ka-un-tŏ nŭn ŏ-di-in-ga-yo?

Where is the check-in counter?

09 부산까지 가시죠?
bu-san gga-ji ga-shi-jyo?

You are going to Busan, right?

10 직항이죠?
jik-hang i-jyo?

It's a direct flight, right?

11 어떤 목적으로 가시나요?
ŏ-ttŏn mok-jŏg ŭ-ro ga-shi-na-yo?

(Lit) For what purpose are you going?

= What's the purpose of your trip?

12 짐을/수하물을 부치시나요?
jim ŭl / su-ha-mul ŭl bu-chi-shi-na-yo?

Are you checking in bags / luggage?

13 짐이/수하물이 몇개인가요?
jim i / su-ha-mul i myŏt-gae-in-ga-yo?

How many bags / luggage is it?

14 짐은/수하물은 무게 제한이 얼마죠?
jim ŭn / su-ha-mul ŭn mu-ge je-han i ŏl-ma-jyo?

What's the weight limit (on the) baggage / luggage?

15 짐이 무게를 초과했어요.
jim i mu-ge rŭl cho-gwa-hae-ssŏ-yo.

(Your) baggage is over the weight (limit).

16 몇개를 뺄게요.
myŏt-gae rŭl bbael-gge-yo.

I'll take out a few.

17 얼마나 초과되었나요?
ŏl-ma-na cho-gwa-doe-ŏt-na-yo?

How much is it over by?

18 이제 어떤가요?
i-je ŏ-ttŏn-ga-yo?

How about now?

19 수속 하셨나요?
su-sok ha-shŏt-na-yo?

Have you checked in?

20 아니요, 수속 좀 도와주세요.
a-ni-yo, su-sok jom do-wa-ju-se-yo.

No, please help me a little (with) check-in.

21 인터넷으로 예약을 했어요.
in-tŏ-ne-sŭ-ro ye-yag ŭl hae-ssŏ-yo.

I made a reservation through the Internet.

22 여기 제 예약번호가 있습니다.
yŏ-gi je ye-yak-bŏn-ho ga it-ssŭp-ni-da.

Here is my reservation number.

23 마일리지가 적립되었습니다.
ma-il-li-ji ga jŏng-nip-doe-ŏ-ssŭp-ni-da.

Mileage has been accumulated.

24 초과 수화물 비용이 있나요?
cho-gwa su-hwa-mul bi-yong i it-na-yo?

Is there a fee (for) excess baggage?

25 카트는 어디 있나요?
ka-tŭ nŭn ŏ-di it-na-yo?

Where are the carts?

26 좌석이 지정되어 있나요?
jwa-sŏg i ji-jŏng-doe-ŏ it-na-yo?

Are the seats pre-assigned?

27 제 좌석은 어디죠?
je jwa-sŏg ŭn ŏ-di-jyo?

Where is my seat?

28 좌석 변경이 가능한가요?
jwa-sŏk byŏn-gyŏng i ga-nŭng-han-ga-yo?

Can I change the seat?

29 창가쪽/복도쪽/가운데 좌석 있나요?
chang-gga-jjok/bok-ddo-jjok/ga-un-dae jwa-sŏk it-na-yo?

Do you have a(n) window/isle/middle seat available?

30 창가쪽/복도쪽/가운데 좌석
부탁합니다.
chang-gga-jjok/bok-ddo-jjok/ga-un-dae jwa-sŏg
bu-tak-hap-ni-da.

A(n) window/isle/middle seat, please.

31 정시에 출발하나요?
jŏng-shi e chul-bal ha-na-yo?

Does it depart at the scheduled time?

32 동반자가 있나요?
dong-ban-ja ga it-na-yo?

Do you have a companion?

33 비자가 있나요?
bi-za ga it-na-yo?

Do you have a visa?

34 신분증을 보여주세요.
shin-bun-tzŭng ŭl bo-yŏ-ju-se-yo.

Show me (your) card, please.

35 몇시에 탑승 시작하죠?
myŏ-sshi-e tap-sŭng shi-jag-ha-jyo?

At what time does the boarding start?

36 만석입니다.
man-sŏg ip-ni-da.

All seats are filled. = We have a full flight.

37 탑승권을 보여주세요.
tap-sŭng-ggwŏn ul bo-yŏ-ju-se-yo.

Show me (your) boarding pass, please.

38 한국항공 카운터는 어디죠?
han-guk-hang-gong ka-un-tŏ nŭn ŏ-di-jyo?

Where is the counter for Hanguk Airline?

39 짐은 어디에서 찾나요?
jim ŭn ŏ-di e-sŏ chat-na-yo?

(From) Where do I find (=pick up) (my) baggage?

40 짐을 잃어버렸어요.
jim-ŭl il-ŏ-bŏ-ryŏ-ssŏ-yo.

I lost (my) baggage.

41 면세점은 어디죠?
myŏn-se-jŏm ŭn ŏ-di-jyo?

Where is the duty-free shop?

42 애완동물도 탑승이 가능한가요?
ae-wan-dong-mul do tap-sŭng-i ga-nŭng-han-ga-yo?

(Lit) Can pets come aboard, too? = Can pets fly, too?

43 환승 게이트는 어디죠?
hwan-sŭng ge-i-tŭ-nŭn ŏ-di-jyo?

Where is the transfer gate?

44 연착 되었나요?
yŏn-chak doe-ŏt-na-yo?

Is it delayed?

45 다음 비행기편에 늦었습니다.
da-ŭm bi-haeng-gi-pyŏn e nŭ-zŏt-ssŭp-ni-da.

(I'm) late to the next flight. = I'm late for (my) connecting flight.

46 비행기를 놓칠 것 같아요.
bi-haeng-gi rŭl not-chil-gŏt gat-a-yo.

I think I'm going to miss (my) airplane (= flight).

47 제가 먼저 가도 될까요?
je ga mŏn-jŏ ga-do doel-gga-yo?

May I go first?

48 줄이 기네요.
jul i gi-ne-yo.

(Lit) The line is long. = It's a long line.

49 여행자보험을 구입하고 싶은데요.
yŏ-haeng-ja bo-hŏm-ŭl gu-ip-ha-go ship-ŭn-de-yo.

I'd like to purchase traveler's insurance.

50 면세품을 주문하고 싶은데요.
myǒn-se-pum ǔl ju-mun-ha-go ship-ǔn-de-yo.

I'd like to order duty-free items.

51 여권을 집에 놓고 왔어요.
yǒ-ggwǒn-ǔl jib e not-ko wa-ssǒ-yo.

(Lit) I came (with my) passport left at home.

52 금지된 물건이 있나요?
gǔm-ji-doen mul-gǒn i it-na-yo?

Are there (any) restricted items?

53 깨지기 쉬운 물건이 들어있어요.
ggae-ji-gi shwi-un mul-gǒn i dǔl-ǒ-i-ssǒ-yo.

There are fragile items in it.

54 짐이 서울까지 가나요?
jim i sǒ-ul gga-ji ga-na-yo?

Does (my) baggage go to Seoul?

55 도쿄까지 연결되나요?
to-kyo gga-ji yǒn-gyǒl-doe-na-yo?

Does it connect to Tokyo?

56 짐을 다시 찾아야 하나요?
jim ǔl da-shi cha-ja-ya ha-na-yo?

Do I have to find (= pick up) (my) baggage again?

57 게이트가 몇번인가요?
ge-i-tǔ ga myǒt bǒn in-ga-yo?

What number is the gate?

58 짐을 부치시겠어요?
jim ǔl bu-chi-shi-get-ssǒ-yo?

Would you like to check in (your) bag?

59 아니요, 들고 탈게요.
a-ni-yo, dǔl-go tal-gge-yo.

No, I will carry it on board.

60 아기도 티켓을 사야 하나요?
a-gi do ti-ke sǔl sa-ya ha-na-yo?

Does a(n) baby/infant have to buy a ticket, too?

61 아기가 몇 살이죠?
a-gi ga myǒt sal i-jyo?

How old is the baby?

62 세 살입니다.
se sal ip-ni-da.

He/She is three years old.

63 신발을/안경을 벗어야 하나요?
shin-bal ǔl/an-gyǒng ǔl bǒ-sǒ-ya ha-na-yo?

Do I need to take off (my) shoes/glasses?

64 랩탑을 꺼내야 하나요?
leb-tab ŭl ggŏ-nae-ya ha-na-yo?

Do I need to take out (my) laptop?

65 모자를 벗어주세요.
mo-ja rŭl bŏ-sŏ-ju-se-yo.

Please take off (your) hat.

66 안경도 벗어야 하나요?
an-gyŏng do bŏ-sŏ-ya ha-na-yo?

Do I need to take off (my) glasses, too?

67 탑승을 시작합니다.
tap-sŭng ŭl shi-jak-hap-ni-da.

(Lit) (We) start boarding. =

We will begin boarding.

68 탑승을 마감합니다.
tap-sŭng ŭl ma-gam-hap-ni-da.

(Lit) (We) close boarding. =

We will close the flight.

69 제가 먼저 왔는데요.
je ga mŏn-jŏ wat-nŭn-de-yo.

(Lit) I came before (you).
= I was here first.

70 줄이 여기인가요?
jul i yŏ-gi in-ga-yo?

(Lit) Is here the line? = Is this the line?

71 도와주시겠어요?
do-wa-ju-si-get-ssŏ-yo?.

Would you please help?

72 비행기를 놓쳤어요.
bi-haeng-gi rŭl not-chŏ-ssŏ-yo.

(I) missed (my) airplane (= flight).

73 연결편이 연착/취소되었어요.
yŏn-gyŏl-pyŏn i yŏn-chak/chwi-so doe-ŏ-ssŏ-yo.

Connecting flight has been delayed/canceled.

74 비행기가 연착/취소되었어요.
bi-haeng-gi ga yŏn-chak/chwi-so doe-ŏ-ssŏ-yo.

The airplane (= flight) has been delayed/canceled.

75 보상을 원합니다.
bo-sang ŭl wŏn-hap-ni-da.

I want compensation.

76 호텔을 제공해주세요.
ho-tel ŭl je-gong hae-ju-se-yo.

Provide me with a hotel, please.

77 남은 자리가 있나요?
nam-ŭn ja-ri ga it-na-yo?

Do you have remaining seats?

78 자리가 다 찼네요.
ja-ri ga da chat-ne-yo.

The seats have been all filled.
= All seats have been filled.

79 편도입니까? 왕복입니까?
pyŏn-do ip-ni-gga? / wang-bog ip-ni-gga?

Is it a one-way? Is it a round trip?

80 편도는/왕복은 얼마죠?
pyŏn-do nŭn / wang-bog ŭn ŏl-ma-jyo?

How much is it for a one-way / round trip?

81 가장 빠른 다음 편은 언제죠?
ga-jang bba-rŭn da-ŭm pyŏn ŭn ŏn-je-jyo?

When is the fastest (= earliest) next flight?

82 짐이 도착을 안했어요.
jim i do-chag ŭl an-hae-ssŏ-yo.

(My) baggage hasn't arrived.

83 가방이 부숴졌어요.
ga-bang i bu-swŏ-jyŏ-ssŏ-yo.

(My) bag has been damaged/broken.

84 지갑이 없어졌어요.
ji-gab i op-ssŏ-jyŏ-ssŏ-yo.

(My) wallet is missing.

85 환전을 하고 싶은데요.
hwan-jŏn ŭl ha-go ship-ŭn-de-yo.

I'd like to exchange money.

86 환율이 어떻게 되나요?
hwan-yul i ŏ-ttŏ-ke doe-na-yo?

What's the exchange rate?

87 10만원 어치 바꿔주세요.
ship ma-wŏn ŏ-chi ba-ggwŏ-ju-se-yo.

Please exchange 100,000 Won's worth.

88 원으로/달러로 바꿔주세요.
wŏn ŭ-ro / dal-lŏ ro ba-ggwŏ-ju-se-yo.

Please exchange it to Won/Dollar.

89 버스는/택시는 어디에서 타나요?
bŏ-sŭ nŭn/tek-shi nŭn ŏ-di-e-sŏ ta-na-yo?

(From) where do I take the bus/taxi?

90 미국까지 가나요?
mi-guk gga-ji ga-na-yo?

Does it go to the U.S.A?

Chapter 7. ON THE PLANE

01 여기 제 자리 같은데요.
yŏ-gi je ja-ri gat-ŭn-de-yo?

I think here (= this) is my seat.
= I think this is me.

02 자리를 확인 해 주시겠어요?
ja-ri rŭl hwag-in hae ju-shi-get-ssŏ-yo?

Would please check (your) seat?

03 자리 찾는 것 좀 도와주세요.
ja-ri chat-nŭn gŏt jom do-wa-ju-se-yo.

Please help me a little (with) finding (my) seat.

04 여기는 제 자리입니다.
yŏ-gi nŭn je ja-ri ip-ni-da.

This is my seat.

05 여권과 탑승권을 보여주세요.
yŏ-ggwŏn-gwa tap-sŭng-gwŏn ŭl bo-yŏ-ju-se-yo.

Please show me (your) passport and boarding pass.

06 들고 타도 되나요?
dŭl-go ta-do doe-na-yo?

Can I carry (this) on?

07 강아지가/고양이가 있어요.
gang-a-ji ga / go-yang-i ga i-ssŏ-yo.

I have a puppy (dog) / cat.

08 짐을 실어주세요.
jim ŭl shil-ŏ-ju-se-yo.

Please load (my) baggage.

09 짐이 무겁습니다.
jim i mu-gŏp-sŭp-ni-da.

(My) baggage is heavy.

10 짐을 꺼내주세요.
jim ŭl ggŏ-nae-ju-se-yo.
Please take out (my) baggage.

11 좀 도와주시겠어요?
jom do-wa-ju-shi-get-ssŏ-yo?
Could you please hele me a little?

12 가방 안에 무엇이 들어있나요?
ga-bang an-e mu-ŏ shi dŭl-ŏ-it-na-yo?
What is in the bag?

13 비상구는 어디입니까?
bi-sang-gu nŭn ŏ-di-ip-ni-gga?
Where is the emergency exit?

14 벨트를 매 주세요.
bel-tŭ rŭl mae ju-se-yo.
Please fasten (your) seat belt.

15 기내에서는 금연입니다.
gi-nae-e-sŏ nŭn gŭm-yŏn-ip-ni-da.
(Lit) It's non-smoking inside the plane.
= Smoking is prohibited on board.

16 휴대폰은 비행기 모드로 바꿔주세요.
hyu-dae-pon ŭn bi-haeng-gi mo-dŭ ro ba-ggwŏ-ju-se-yo.
Please switch (your) cell phone to airplane mode.

17 전자기기를 모두 꺼주세요.
jŏn-ja-gi-gi rŭl mo-du ggŏ-ju-se-yo.
Please turn off all (your) electronic devices.

18 휴대폰을 써도 되나요?
hyu-dae-pon ŭl ssŏ-do doe-na-yo?
Can I use (my) cell phone?

19 화장실에 가도 되나요?
hwa-jang-shil e ga-do doe-na-yo?
Can I go to the restroom?

20 승무원의 안내에 따라주세요.
sŭng-mu-wŏn ŭi an-nae-e tta-ra-ju-se-yo.
Please follow (to/by) the flight attendant's directions.

21 등받이를 세워주세요.
dŭng-ba-ji rŭl se-wŏ-ju-se-yo.
Please pull up the recliner (= seat).

22 창문을 올려주세요.
chang-mun-ŭl ol-lyŏ-ju-se-yo.
Please roll up the window.

23 기류가 불안정합니다.
gi-ryu ga bul-an-jŏng-hap-ni-da.

(Lit) The airstream is unstable.

= We are experiencing turbulence.

24 자리로 돌아가주세요.
ja-ri ro dol-a-ga-ju-se-yo.

Please return to (your) seat.

25 언제 출발하나요?
ŏn-je chul-bal ha-na-yo?

When do (we) depart = (take off)?

26 언제 도착하나요?
ŏn-je do-chak ha-na-yo?

When do (we) arrive?

27 기내식은 언제 나오나요?
gi-nae-shig ŭn ŏn-je na-o-na-yo?

(Lit) When do the (in-flight) meals come out?

= When are the inflight meals served?

28 메뉴를 볼 수 있을까요?
me-nyu rŭl bol su i-ssŭl-gga-yo?

May I see the menu?

29 알러지가 있으신가요?
al-lŏ-ji ga i-ssŭ-shin-ga-yo?

Do you have allergies?

30 땅콩에 알러지가 있습니다.
ttang-kong e al-lŏ-j i ga it-ssŭp-ni-da.

(Lit) I have allergies to peanuts.

= I'm allergic to peanuts.

31 식사를 드리겠습니다.
shik-sa rŭl dŭ-ri-get-ssŭp-ni-da.

We will give (= serve) you the meals.

32 어느 것으로 하시겠습니까?
ŏ-nŭ gŏ sŭ-ro ha-shi-get-ssŭm-ni-gga?

Which one would you like to go (with)?

33 식사를 바꿔도 되나요?
shik-sa rŭl ba-ggwŏ-do doe-na-yo?

Can I change (my) meal?

34 기내식이 나올때 깨워주세요.
gi-nae-shig i na-ol-ttae ggae-wŏ-ju-se-yo.

Please wake me up when the (in-flight) meals come out (= are served).

35 머리가 아파요.
mŏ-ri ga a-pa-yo.

(My) head aches.

36 두통이 심합니다.
du-tong i shim-hap-ni-da.

(Lit) Headache is severe.

I have a severe headache.

37 토할 것 같아요.
to-hal gŏt gat-a-yo.

I think I'm going to throw up.

38 멀미가 심하네요.
mŏl-mi ga shim-ha-ne-yo.

(Lit) (My) airsickness is severe.

I'm getting very airsick.

39 속이 좋지 않아요.
sog i jot-chi a-na-yo.

(Lit) (My) inside is not good.

= My stomach is upset.

40 진통제 있나요?
jin-tong-je it-na-yo?

Do you have a painkiller?

41 비행기안에 의사가 있나요?
bi-haeng-gi an-e ŭi-sa ga it-na-yo?

Is there a doctor inside (= on) the plane?

42 충전이 가능한가요?
chung-jŏn i ga-nŭng-han-ga-yo?

Is it possible to charge (the phone)?

43 팔걸이가 고장났어요.
pal-gŏl-i ga go-jang-na-ssŏ-yo.

The armrest is broken.

44 리모콘이 작동을 안해요.
ri-mo-kon i jak-dong ŭl an-hae-yo.

The remote isn't working.

45 엔진에서 연기가 나요.
en-jin e-sŏ yŏn-gi ga na-yo.

Smoke is coming out of the engine.

46 비상사태입니다.
bi-sang-sa-tae ip-ni-da.

It's an emergency situation.

47 의자가 고장났어요.
ŭi-ja ga go-jang-na-ssŏ-yo.

The chair (= seat) is broken.

48 불이 안 켜져요.
bul i an kyŏ-jyŏ-yo.

The light doesn't turn on.

49 티비를 어떻게 사용하죠?
ti-bi rŭl ŏ-ttŏ-gge sa-yong-ha-jyo?

How do I use the TV?

50 티비가 안나와요.
ti-bi ga an-na-wa-yo.

(Lit) TV doesn't come on. = TV doesn't work.

51 저 승객이 이상해요.
jŏ sŭng-gaeg i i-sang-hae-yo.
That passenger is weird/strange.

52 많이 취한 것 같아요.
man-i chwi-han gŏt gat-a-yo.
(He/She) seems very drunk.

53 다른 자리로 옮겨도 될까요?
da-rŭn ja-ri ro om-gyŏ-do doel-gga-yo?
Can I switch to a different seat?

54 빨리 내려야 해요.
bbal-li nae-ryŏ-ya hae-yo.
I have to get off quickly.

55 어디까지 가세요?
ŏ-di gga-ji ga-se-yo?
(Lit) How far are you going?
= Where's your final destination?

56 저도 거기에 갑니다.
jŏ do gŏ-gi e gap-ni-da.
I am going (to) there too.

57 여행 가시나요?
yŏ-haeng ga-shi-na-yo?
Are you going (on a) trip?

58 코를 골아서 죄송합니다.
ko rŭl gol-a-sŏ joe-song-hap-ni-da.
(Lit) Sorry for snoring (my nose).

59 안대 있나요?
an-dae it-na-yo?
Do you have a sleep shade?

60 담요를 주세요.
dam-nyo rŭl ju-se-yo.
Please give me a blanket.

61 물 좀 주세요.
mul jom ju-se-yo.
Give me some water, please.

62 심하게 흔들리네요.
shim-ha-ge hŭn-dŭl-li-ne-yo.
It's shaking excessively.

63 면세품은 어디서 찾나요?
myŏn-se-pum ŭn ŏ-di-sŏ chat-na-yo?
(From) where do I pick up duty-free items?

64 면세 한도가 어떻게 되나요?
myŏn-se han-do ga ŏ-ttŏ-ke doe-na-yo?
What's the duty-free limit?

65 이것을 사고 싶어요.
i-gŏ sŭl sa-go ship-ŏ-yo.

I'd like to buy this.

66 여기 있습니다.
yŏ-gi it-ssŭp-ni-da.

Here you are.

67 필요한게 있으면 알려주세요.
pil-yo-han-ge i-ssŭ-myŏn al-lyŏ-ju-se-yo.

Please let me know
if there is anything you need.

68 현지 시각은 몇시죠?
hyŏn-ji shi-gag ŭn myŏ-sshi-jyo?

What time is the local time (now)?

69 입국신고서를 작성해주세요.
ip-guk-shin-go-sŏ rŭl jak-sŏng hae-ju-se-yo.

Please fill out the arrival card.

70 세관 신고서를 작성 해주세요.
se-gwan shin-go-sŏ rŭl jak-sŏng hae-ju-se-yo.

Please fill out
the customs declaration form.

Chapter 8. VISA & IMMIGRATION

01 어떤 일로 오셨나요?
ŏ-ttŏn il lo o-shŏt-na-yo?

(Lit) What kind of matter did you come (here) for?

= How may I help you?

02 비자를 갱신하려고요.
bi-za rŭl gaeng-shin ha-ryŏ-go-yo.

I'd like to get (my) visa renewed.

03 비자가 만기되었어요.
bi-za ga man-gi doe-ŏ-ssŏ-yo.

(My/Your) visa has expired.

04 어떤 비자를 갖고 계시죠?
ŏ-ttŏn bi-za rŭl gat-go gye-shi-jyo?

What kind of visa do you have?

= What's your visa status?

05 관광/투자/학생 비자입니다.
gwan-gwang/tu-ja/hak-saeng bi-za ip-ni-da.

It's a tourist/investor/student visa.

06 영주권자인가요?
yŏng-ju-gwŏn-ja in-ga-yo?

Are you a permanent resident?

07 어느 나라 국적이시죠?
ŏ-nŭ na-ra guk-jŏk i-shi-jyo?

(Lit) What country nationality are you?

= What's your nationality?

08 신청서를 작성해주세요.
shin-chiŏng-sŏ rŭl jak-sŏng hae-ju-se-yo.

Please fill out the application.

09 서류가 부족합니다.
sŏ-ryu-ga bu-jok-hap-ni-da.

(Lit) Documents are insufficient.

You are missing some documents.

10 서류가 빠진 것 같아요.
sŏ-ryu ga bba-jin gŏt gat-a-yo.

It seems like documents are missing.

11 신청서가 통과되지 못했습니다.
shin-chŏng-sŏ ga tong-gwa-doe-ji mot-haet-sŭp-ni-da.

(Your) application didn't go through.

12 신청서가 통과되었습니다.
shin-chŏng-sŏ ga tong-gwa doe-ŏt-ssŭp-ni-da.

(Your) application did go through.

13 다시 작성해주세요.
da-shi jak-sŏng hae-ju-se-yo.

Please fill it out again.

14 담당자가 자리에 없습니다.
dam-dang-ja ga ja-ri-e ŏp-sŭp-ni-da.

(Lit) The person in charge isn't in (his) seat.

= The person in charge is away.

15 어디 한번 볼까요?
ŏ-di han-bŏn bol-gga-yo?

Shall we take a look?

16 빠진게 없는지 확인해보세요.
bba-jin-ge ŏp-nŭn-ji hwag-in hae-bo-se-yo.

Please check if there isn't anything missing.

17 이렇게 작성하면 되나요?
i-rŏt-ke jak-sŏng ha-myŏn doe-na-yo?

(Lit) Is this okay if I fill out like this?

= Can I fill it out like this?

18 어떻게 작성해야 하나요?
ŏ-ttŏ-ke jak-sŏng hae-ya ha-na-yo?

How should I fill it out?

19 이 부분이 잘 이해가 안됩니다.
i bu-bun i jal i-hae ga an-doep-ni-da.

I don't quite understand this part.

20 필요한 서류는 무엇인가요?
pil-yo-han sŏ-ryu nŭn mu-ŏ-shin-ga-yo?

What are the necessary/required documents?

21 어느 부서로 가면 될까요?
ŏ-nŭ bu-sŏ ro ga-myŏn doel-gga-yo?

Which department should I go to?

22 오늘 중으로 처리 될까요?
o-nŭl jung-ŭ-ro chŏ-ri doel-gga-yo?

Will it be processed within today?

23 택배로 보내주세요.
tek-bae-ro bo-nae-ju-se-yo.

Please send (it) by courier service.

24 자리에서 대기해 주세요.
ja-ri-e-sŏ dae-gi hae ju-se-yo.

Please wait from (=at) (your) seat.

25 번호표를 뽑아주세요.
bŏn-ho-pyo rŭl bbob-a ju-se-yo.

Please pick (= take) a number ticket.

26 아직 차례가 아닙니다.
a-jik cha-rye ga a-nip-ni-da.

It's not (your) turn yet.

27 온라인으로도 신청 가능합니다.
on-la-in ŭ-ro do shin-chŏng ga-nŭng-hap-ni-da.

(Lit) It's possible to submit it by online as well.

=You can submit it online as well.

28 내일 다시 오세요.
nae-il da-shi o-se-yo.

Please come again tomorrow.

29 며칠 정도 걸릴까요?
myŏ-chil jŏng-do gŏl-lil-gga-yo?

About how many days (= long) would it take?

30 통역이 있나요?
tong-yŏk i it-na-yo?

Do you have an interpreter?

31 공증을 받아야 합니다.
gong-zŭng ŭl bad-a ya hap-ni-da.

You need to have it notarized.

32 인터뷰를 해야합니다.
in-tŏ-byu rŭl hae-ya-hap-ni-da.

You need to do an interview.

33 변호사가 동행해도 되나요?
byŏn-ho-sa ga dong-haeng hae-do doe-na-yo?

Can a lawyer/attorney accompany me?

34 귀화를 신청하고 싶습니다.
gwi-hwa rŭl shin-chŏng ha-go-ship-ssŭp-ni-da.

I'd like to file (for) naturalization.

35 귀화 절차는 어떻게 되나요?
gwi-hwa jŏl-cha nŭn ŏ-ttŏ-ke doe-na-yo?

What's the process (for) naturalization?

36 이중국적이 허용되나요?
i-jung guk-jŏg i hŏ-yong-doe-na-yo?

Is dual citizenship allowed?

37 여권이 만료되었어요.
yŏ-ggwŏn i mal-lyo-doe-ŏt-ŏ-yo.

(My/Your) passport has expired.

38 사진이 필요합니다.
sa-jin i pil-yo-hap-ni-da.

You need a photo.

39 수수료가 얼마죠?
su-su-ryo ga ŏl-ma-jyo?

How much is the fee?

40 검색대를 통과해야 합니다.
gŏm-saek-dae rŭl tong-gwa hae-ya hap-ni-da.

You need to go through the scanner.

41 소지품은 여기에 맡기세요.
so-ji-pum ŭn yŏ-gi e mat-gi-se-yo.

Please leave (your) belongings here.

42 나가실때 찾으세요.
na-ga-shil-ttae cha-zŭ-se-yo.

Find them (pick them up) when you leave.

43 함께 들어가도 되나요?
ham-gge dŭl-ŏ-ga-do doe-na-yo?

Can I go in together?

44 서류가 처리되었습니다.
sŏ-ryu ga chŏ-ri doe-ŏt-ssŭp-ni-da.

Documents have been processed.

45 승인/거절되었습니다.
sŭng-in/gŏ-jŏl doe-ŏt-ssŭp-ni-da.

It's been approved/rejected (= denied).

46 한국에서 하시는 일이 뭐죠?
han-guk e-sŏ ha-shi-nŭn il i mwŏ-jyo?

(Lit) What is the work you do in Korea?

47 어디에서 일하고 계시죠?
ŏ-di e-sŏ il-ha-go gye-shi-jyo?

Where are (you) working at?

48 한국에 얼마나 머무실 예정인가요?
han-gug e ŏl-ma-na mŏ-mu-shil ye-jŏng-in-ga-yo?

How long do you plan to stay in Korea?

49 면세한도를 초과한 물품이 있나요?
myŏn-se-han-do-rŭl cho-gwa-han mul-pum i it-na-yo?

Do you have items that are over the customs limit?

50 금지된 품목이 있나요?
gŭm-ji-doen pum-mog i it-na-yo?

Do you have prohibited items?

51 한국 방문 목적이 어떻게 되시죠?
han-gug bang-mun mok-jŏg i ŏ-ttŏ-ke doe-shi-jyo?

What's the purpose (of your) visit (to) Korea?

52 한국에서는 어디에 머무르시죠?
han-guk e-sŏ nŭn ŏ-di-e mŏ mu-rŭ-shi-jyo?

(At) where are you staying in Korea?

53 관광 목적으로 왔습니다.
gwan-gwang mok-jŏg ŭ-ro wat-ssŭp-ni-da.

I came for the purpose (of) sightseeing.

54 한국호텔에 머무릅니다.
han-guk ho-tel e mŏ-mu-rŭp-ni-da.

I'm staying at Hanguk hotel.

55 짐은 이게 전부입니다.
jim ŭn i-ge jŏn-bu ip-ni-da.

This is all (for my) baggage.

56 홍대에서 공부하고 있습니다.
hong-dae e-sŏ gong-bu ha-go-it-ssŭp-ni-da.

I'm studying at Hongdae.

57 약 6개월 머무를 예정입니다.
yak yuk-gae-wŏl mŏ-mu-rŭl ye-jŏng-ip-ni-da.

I plan to stay (for) about 6 months.

58 보증인의 편지입니다.
bo-zŭng-in-ŭi pyŏn-ji ip-ni-da.

(This) is a letter (from my) guarantor.

59 2차 심사실로 가주세요.
i-cha shim-sa-shil ro ga-ju-se-yo.

Please go to the secondary screening room.

60 이제 다 되셨습니다.
i-je da doe-shŏt-ssŭp-ni-da.

(Lit) It's all set now.

61 가보셔도 좋습니다.
ga-bo-shŏ-do jot-ssŭp-ni-da.

(Lit) It's fine for you to go.

= You may go now. / You are good to go.

62 즐거운 여행 되세요.
jŭl-gŏ-un yŏ-haeng doe-se-yo.

Have a pleasant trip.

Chapter 9. TAXI

01 택시!
tek-shi!

Taxi!

02 반포까지 가주세요.
banpo gga-ji ga-ju-se-yo.

Please go to Banpo.

03 반포에 가려고 하는데요.
banpo e ga-ryǒ-go ha-nǔn-de-yo.

I'm trying to get to Banpo.

04 주소를 보여 드릴게요.
ju-so rǔl bo-yǒ dǔ-ril-gge-yo.

Let me show you the address.

05 이게 주소입니다.
i-ge ju-so ip-ni-da.

This is the address

06 목적지가 어디죠?
mok-jǒk-ji ga ǒ-di-jyo?

Where is the destination?

07 목적지는 여기입니다.
mok-jǒk-ji nǔn yǒ-gi ip-ni-da.

(Lit) Here (= this) is the destination.

08 여기로 가주세요.
yǒ-gi ro ga-ju-se-yo.

(Lit) Please go to here. = Please take me here.

09 어디로 갈까요?
ǒ-di ro gal-gga-yo?

(Lit) To where should we go?

10 빨리 가주세요.
bbal-li ga-ju-se-yo.

Please go quickly. = Step on it, please.

11 빠른 길로 가주세요.
bba-rŭn gil ro ga-ju-se-yo.

(Lit) Please go by the fast route.

12 지름길로 가주세요.
ji-rŭm-gil ro ga-ju-se-yo.

(Lit) Please go by the shortcut.

= Please take the shortcut.

13 여기 세워주세요.
yŏ-gi se-wŏ-ju-se-yo.

(Lit) Please stop it here.

= Please pull over here.

14 여기 내릴게요.
yŏ-gi nae-ril-gge-yo.

I will get off here.

15 수고하세요.
su-go-ha-se-yo.

(Lit) Keep up the good work.

= Thank you / Take it easy / Goodbye.

16 내비를 따라 가주세요.
ne-bi rŭl tta-ra ga-ju-se-yo.

Please follow the navigation.

17 돌아가는 것 같은데요.
dol-a-ga-nŭn gŏt gat-ŭn-de-yo.

I think we are taking a roundabout route.

18 이 길이 아닙니다.
i gil i a-nip-ni-da.

It's not this way.

19 이쪽으로 가면 안돼요.
i-jjog ŭ-ro ga-myŏn an-doe-yo.

You shouldn't go (to) this way.

20 카드로 계산할게요.
ka-dŭ ro gye-san-hal-gge-yo.

I'll pay by (= with) a (credit) card.

21 현금이 없어요.
hyŏn-gŭm i ŏp-ssŏ-yo.

I don't have cash.

22 요금이 너무 많이 나왔어요.
yo-gŭm i nŏ-mu man-i na-wa-ssŏ-yo.

(Lit) The fare came out too much.

= You are overcharging me.

23 경찰서로 갑시다.
gyŏng-chal-sŏ ro gap-shi-da.

Let's go to the police station.

24 이건 아니죠.
i-gŏn a-ni-jyo.

This is not right.

25 외국인이라고 바가지 씌우면 안돼요.
oe-gug-in i-ra-go ba-ga-ji ssi-u-myŏn an-doe-yo.

(Lit) You shouldn't rip me off because I'm a foreigner.

26 직진 해주세요.
jik-jin hae-ju-se-yo.

Please go straight.

27 계속 가주세요.
gye-sok ga-ju-se-yo.

(Lit) Please continue going.
= Please keep going.

28 좌회전/우회전 해주세요.
jwa-hoe-jŏn/u-hoe-jŏn hae-ju-se-yo.

Take a left turn/right turn, please.

29 여기서/저기서 직진 해주세요.
yŏ-gi-sŏ/jŏ-gi-sŏ jik-jin/u-hoe-jŏn hae-ju-se-yo.

Go straight (at) here/there, please.

30 이번/다음 신호등에서 유턴 해주세요.
i-bŏn / da-ŭm shin-ho-dŭng e-sŏ yu-tŏn hae-ju-se-yo.

Make a U-turn at this/next light, please.

31 이번/다음 골목으로 들어가 주세요.
i-bŏn / da-ŭm gol-mog ŭ-ro dŭl-ŏ-ga ju-se-yo.

Go into this/next alley, please.

32 지나쳤어요.
ji-na-chyŏ-ssŏ-yo.

You've passed it.

33 너무 많이 왔어요.
nŏ-mu man-i wa-ssŏ-yo.

You've come too much (= far).

34 여기가 아닌데요.
yŏ-gi ga a-nin-de-yo.

(Lit) Here (= This) isn't (the place).

35 아까 거기로 돌아가 주세요.
a-gga gŏ-gi ro dol-a-ga ju-se-yo.

(Lit) Please go back to that place (= where we were) before.

36 목적지가 바뀌었어요.
mok-jŏk-ji ga ba-ggwi-ŏ-ssŏ-yo.

The destination has been changed.

37 통역을 부탁합니다.
tong-yŏg ŭl bu-tak-hap-ni-da.
I'd like a translator, please.

38 영수증을 주세요.
yŏng-su-zŭng ŭl ju-se-yo.
Please give me the receipt.

39 신고 할거예요.
shin-go hal-gŏ-ye-yo.
I'm going to report you.

40 트렁크 좀 열어주세요.
tŭ-rŏng-kŭ jom yŏl-ŏ-ju-se-yo.
Please open the trunk for me?

41 트렁크에 짐 좀 넣을게요.
tŭ-rŏn-kŭ e jim jom nŏ-ŭl-gge-yo.
I'm going to put some baggage in the trunk.

42 요금이 정해져 있나요?
yo-gŭm i jŏng-hae-jyŏ it-na-yo?
(Lit) Is the fare fixed/pre-determined?
= Is it a flat fare?

43 미터기로 갑니다.
mi-tŏ-gi ro gap-ni-da.
(Lit) It goes by the taxi meter.
= It's charged by the taxi meter.

44 열시 까지 도착할 수 있을까요?
yŏl-shi gga-ji do-chak-hal su i-ssŭl-gga-yo?
Can we arrive by 10 o'clock?

45 고속도로를 타주세요.
go-sok-do-ro rŭl ta-ju-se-yo.
Please ride (= take) the highway.

46 추가 요금이 있습니다.
chu-ga yo-gŭm i it-ssŭp-ni-da.
There is an additional charge.

47 창문 좀 열어주세요.
chang-mun jom yŏl-ŏ-ju-se-yo.
Please open the window (for me).

48 창문 좀 닫아주세요.
chang-mun jom dad-a-ju-se-yo.
Please close the window (for me).

49 잔돈은 괜찮습니다.
jan-don-ŭn goen-chan-sŭp-ni-da.
Don't worry about the change.
= Keep the change.

50 여기 왼쪽/오른쪽.
yŏ-gi oen-jjog/o-rŭn-jjog-i-yo.
(On the) left/right here.

51 내릴게요.
nae-ril-gge-yo.

Let me get off

52 택시 좀 불러주세요.
tek-shi jom bul-lŏ-ju-se-yo.

Please call a taxi for me.

53 이 주소로 가주세요.
i ju-so ro ga-ju-se-yo.

Please go to this address (for me).

54 트렁크에 가방 좀 넣어주세요.
tŭ-rŏn-kŭ e ga-bang jom nŏ-ŏ-ju-se-yo.

Please put the bag in the trunk (for me).

55 이태원까지는 얼마 나올까요?
i-tae-wŏn gga-ji nŭn ŏl-ma na-ol-gga-yo?

How much would it cost (to get) to Itaewon?

56 좀 바쁩니다.
jom ba-bbŭp-ni-da.

I am in a bit of a hurry.

57 택시는 어디에서 타나요?
tek-shi-nŭn ŏ-di-e-sŏ ta-na-yo?

Where can I get a taxi?

58 택시 번호를 가지고 계세요?
tek-shi bŏn-ho rŭl ga-ji-go gye-se-yo?

Do you have the taxi number?

59 다 왔나요?
da wat-na-yo?

(Lit) Have we come fully?

Are we there?

60 이태원으로 데리러 올 수 있나요?
i-tae-wŏn ŭ-ro de-ri-rŏ ol su it-na-yo?

Can you come to Itaewon to pick me up?

61 가는 중입니다.
ga-nŭn jung-ip-ni-da.

(Lit) I'm in the middle (of) going.

= I'm on my way.

62 여기서 기다려 주실 수 있나요?
yŏ-gi-sŏ gi-da-ryŏ ju-shil su it-na-yo?

Can you wait for me (from) here, please?

63 미터기가 작동하고 있나요?
mi-tŏ-gi ga jak-dong ha-go it-na-yo?

Is the taxi meter working?

64 미터기를 켜 주세요.
mi-tŏ-gi rŭl kyŏ ju-se-yo.

Please turn on the taxi meter.

65 천천히 말해주세요.
chŏn-chŏn-hi mal-hae-ju-se-yo.

Please speak slowly.

66 백화점에서 내려주세요.
bae-kwa-jŏ-m-e-so nae-ryo-ju-se-yo.

Please drop me off at the department store.

67 천천히 가주세요.
chŏn-chŏn-hi ga-ju-se-yo.

Please go (= drive) slowly.

68 에어컨을 켜주세요/꺼주세요.
e-ŏ-kŏn ŭl kyo-ju-se-yo/ggŏ-ju-se-yo.

Please turn on/off the A/C.

69 방향을 저쪽으로 바꿔주세요.
bang-hyang ŭl jŏ-jjog ŭ-ro ba-ggwo-ju-se-yo.

Please change the direction to that way.

70 편의점에 들렀다가 갈게요.
pyŏn-ŭi-jŏm e dŭl-lŏt-da-ga gal-gge-yo.

(Lit) I'll go after stopping by the convenience store.

71 가다가 일행을 태우고 가야합니다.
ga-da-ga il-haeng ŭl tae-u-go ga-ya-hap-ni-da.

(Lit) I need to go after picking up a companion on the way.

Chapter 10. SUBWAY/METRO

01 지하철역이 어디죠?
ji-ha-chŏl yŏg i   ŏ-di-jyo?

Where is the subway station?

02 지하철 노선도가 있나요?
ji-ha-chŏl no-sŏn-do ga   it-na-yo?

Do you have a subway line map?

03 지하철 노선을 잘 몰라요.
ji-ha-chŏl no-sŏn ŭl jal   mol-la-yo.

I'm not very familiar with the subway lines.

04 인천까지 가려면 몇호선을 타야 하나요?
in-chŏn gga-ji ga-ryŏ-myŏn myŏt ho-sŏn ŭl ta-ya ha-na-yo?

What number line should I take to get to Incheon?

05 1호선을 타세요.
il ho-sŏn ŭl   ta-se-yo.

Take line number 1.

06 어느 역에서 내려야 하나요?
ŏ-nŭ yŏg e-sŏ   nae-ri-myŏn doe-na-yo?

Which station should I get off of?

07 제가 맞게 탔나요?
je ga mat-ge tat-na-yo?

(Lit) Did I get on right?

= Am I on the right train?

08 개찰구는 어디인가요?
gae-chal-gu nŭn ŏ-di-in-ga-yo?

Where is the ticket gate/turnstile?

09 어떻게 계산하나요?
ŏ-ttŏ-ke   gye-san ha-na-yo?

(Lit) How do I calculate?

= How can I pay?

10 지하철표는 어디서 사나요?
ji-ha-chŏl-pyo nŭn ŏ-di-sŏ sa-na-yo?

Where do I buy the subway ticket?

11 잘못 탄 것 같아요.
jal-mot tan gŏt gat-a-yo.

(Lit) I think I got on wrongly.

= I think I got on the wrong train.

12 반대 방향으로 가는 것 같아요.
ban-dae bang-hyang ŭ-ro ga-nŭn gŏt gat-a-yo.

I think it's going in the opposite direction.

13 어느 쪽으로 내리나요?
ŏ-nŭ jjog ŭ-ro nae-ri-na-yo?

(Lit) To which way do I get off?

= Which way do I get off?

14 출구가 어디죠?
chul-gu ga ŏ-di-jyo?

Where is the exit?

15 몇 번 출구로 나가야 하나요?
myŏt bŏn chul-gu-ro na-ga-ya ha-na-yo?

(Lit) Which number exit should I get out of?

16 몇 정거장 가야 하나요?
myŏt jŏng-gŏ-jang ga-ya ha-na-yo?

How many stations (= stops)

do I have to go?

17 이 방향이 맞나요?
i bang-hyang i mat-na-yo?

Is this direction right?

= Is this the right direction?

18 어디서 내리세요?
ŏ-di-sŏ nae-ri-se-yo?

(From) Where do you get off?

19 어디서 내려야 하나요?
ŏ-di-sŏ nae-ryŏ-ya ha-na-yo?

(From) where should I get off?

20 여기서 내리면 되나요?
yŏ-gi-sŏ nae-ri-myŏn doe-na-yo?

Can I get off (from) here?

= Is this my stop?

21 이번/다음 역에서 내리세요.
i-bŏn/da-ŭm yŏg e-sŏ nae-ri-se-yo.

Get off from (= at) this/next station.

22 환승해야합니다.
hwan-sŭng hae-ya-hap-ni-da.

You need to make a transfer.

23 환승 하려면 어디로 가나요?
hwan-sŭng ha-ryŏ-myŏn ŏ-di-ro ga-na-yo?

(Lit) To where do I go to make a transfer?

24 5호선으로 환승 해야 합니다.
o ho-sŏn ŭ-ro hwan-sŭng hae-ya hap-ni-da.

You need to make a transfer into line number 5.

25 지하철 카드는 어디에서 사나요?
ji-ha-chŏl ka-dŭ nŭn ŏ-di-e-sŏ sa-na-yo?

From where do I buy the subway card?

26 여기서 타면 되나요?
yŏ-gi-sŏ ta-myŏn doe-na-yo?

Should I take (the train) here?

27 줄 서세요.
jul sŏ-se-yo.

(Lit) Please stand in line.

= Please line up.

28 새치기 하지 마세요.
sae-chi-gi ha-ji ma-se-yo.

Don't cut in line, please.

29 발을 밟아서 죄송합니다.
bal ŭl bal-ba-sŏ joe-song-hap-ni-da.

I'm sorry for stepping/trodding (on your) foot (= toes).

30 발을 밟지 마세요.
bal-ŭl bal-jji ma-se-yo.

Please don't step/trod on (my) foot (= toes).

31 자리 좀 만들어 주세요.
ja-ri jom man-dŭl-ŏ ju-se-yo.

Make some space (= room), please.

32 다리를 너무 벌리지 마세요.
da-ri rŭl nŏ-mu bŏl-li-ji ma-se-yo.

Don't spread (your) legs too much.

33 여성 전용 칸 입니다.
yŏ-sŏng jŏn-yong kan ip-ni-da.

It's a "women-only" car.

34 노약자석입니다.
no-yak-ja sŏg ip-ni-da.

It's a seat (for) the old and the disabled.

35 여기 앉으세요.
yŏ-gi an-zŭ-se-yo.

Please sit here.

36 저는 서서 가도 됩니다.
jŏ nŭn sŏ-sŏ ga-do doep-ni-da.

(Lit) I can go by standing.

= I don't mind standing.

37 양보해 주셔서 감사합니다.
yang-bo hae ju-shŏ-sŏ gam-sa-hap-ni-da.
Thanks for offering/yielding.

38 물론이죠.
mul-lo-ni-jyo.
Of course.

39 다리가 많이 아파요.
da-ri ga man-i a-pa-yo.
(My) legs hurt a lot.

40 손잡이를 잡으세요.
son-jab-i rŭl jab-ŭ-se-yo.
Grab the handle.

41 카드 좀 충전 해주세요.
ka-dŭ jom chung-jŏn hae-ju-se-yo.
Please recharge/top up (my) card for me.

42 카드 충전 되나요?
ka-dŭ chung-jŏn doe-na-yo?
Can I recharge/top up (my) card?

43 어디서 갈아타야 하나요?
ŏ-di-sŏ gal-a-ta-ya ha-na-yo?
(From) where can I change the ride?
= Where can I make a transfer?

44 시청에서 갈아타세요.
shi-chŏng e-sŏ gal-a-ta-se-yo.
Change the ride (= make a transfer) at the City Hall.

45 매표소가 어디죠?
mae-pyo-so ga ŏ-di-jyo?
Where is the ticket office?

46 공항까지 가는데 얼마죠?
gong-hang gga-ji ga-nŭn-de ŏl-ma-jyo?
How much is it to get to the airport?

47 몇시가 막차인가요?
myŏ-sshi ga mak-cha in-ga-yo?
What time is the last train?

48 반대 방향으로 건널 수 있나요?
ban-dae bang-hyang ŭ-ro gŏn-nŏl su it-na-yo?
Can I cross over to the opposite side?

49 얼마나 충전 해 드릴까요?
ŏl-ma-na chung-jŏn hae dŭ-ril-gga-yo?
(Lit) How much should I recharge it for you?
= How much do you want to charge?

50 만원 어치 충전 해주세요.
ma-nwŏn ŏ-chi chung-jŏn hae-ju-se-yo.
Recharge 10,000 won's worth, please.

71

51 이번/다음 역은 여의도역 입니다.
i-bŏn / da-ŭm yŏg ŭn yŏ-ŭi-do yŏg ip-ni-da.

This/Next station is Yeuido station.

52 열차가 들어오고 있습니다.
yŏl-cha ga dŭl-ŏ-o-go it-ssŭp-ni-da.

(Lit) The train is coming in.

= The train is approaching.

53 여기서 가장 가까운 역은 어디죠?
yŏ-gi-sŏ ga-jang ga-gga-un yŏg ŭn ŏ-di-jyo?

Where is the nearest station from here?

54 이 근처에 지하철역이 있나요?
i gŭn-chŏ e ji-ha-chŏl yŏg i it-na-yo?

Is there a subway station near here?

55 학생/노인 요금은 얼마죠?
hak-saeng/no-in yo-gŭm ŭn ŏl-ma-jyo?

How much is the fare (for) a student/senior citizen?

56 갈아 타야 하나요?
gal-a ta-ya ha-na-yo?

Do I have to change the ride (= make a transfer)?

57 일회용/하루용/일주일용 카드가 있나요?
il-hoe-yong/ha-ru-yong/il-ju-il-lyong ka-dŭ ga it-na-yo?

Do you have a one-time/daily/weekly card?

58 다음 열차는 몇시에 도착하나요?
da-ŭm yŏl-cha nŭn myŏ-sshi e do-chak-ha-na-yo?

(At) what time does the next train arrive?

59 급행 열차입니다.
gŭp-haeng yŏl-cha ip-ni-da.

It's an express train.

60 이 열차는 역마다 정차하나요?
i yŏl-cha nŭn yŏg-ma-da jŏng-cha-ha-na-yo?

Does this train stop (at) every station?

61 김포까지 멈추지 않고 갑니다.
gim-po gga-ji mŏm-chu-ji an-ko gap-ni-da.

It goes to Gimpo without stopping.

62 열차가 왜 이렇게 늦죠?
yŏl-cha ga oe i-rŏt-ke nŭt-jyo?

Why is the train this late?

63 열차가 곧 출발합니다.
yŏl-cha ga got chul-bal hap-ni-da.

The train is departing soon.

64 이번 역에서 10분간 정차합니다.
i-bŏn yŏg e-sŏ ship-bun-gan jŏng-cha-hap-ni-da.

We will stop for 10 minutes at this station.

65 분실물 센터는 어디인가요?
bun-shil-mul sen-tŏ nŭn ŏ-di-in-ga-yo?

Where is the lost and found (center)?

66 역무원을 불러주세요.
yŏg-mu-wŏn ŭl bul-lŏ-ju-se-yo.

Please call the station staff for me.

67 역무원은 어디 있나요?
yŏg-mu-wŏn ŭn ŏ-di it-na-yo?

Where is the station staff?

Chapter 11. AT THE HOTEL

01 로비는 어디죠?
lo-bi nŭn ŏ-di-jyo?

Where is the lobby?

02 프론트 데스크는 어디인가요?
pŭ-ron-tŭ de-sŭ-kŭ nŭn ŏ-di-n-ga-yo?

Where is the front desk?

03 체크인은 어디에서 하나요?
he-kŭ-in ŭn ŏ-di e-sŏ ha-na-yo?

(Lit) From where do I check-in?

04 짐을 들어드릴까요?
jim-ŭl dŭl-ŏ-dŭ-ril-gga-yo?

Do you want me to carry (your) luggage?

= Do you need help with your bags?

05 트렁크에서 짐을 내려주세요.
tŭ-rŏn-kŭ e-sŏ jim ŭl nae-ryŏ-ju-se-yo.

Please unload the bags from the trunk.

06 주차는 어디에 하나요?
ju-cha nŭn ŏ-di e ha-na-yo?

(Lit) At where do I park?

07 발렛 파킹을 하고 싶은데요.
bal-let-pa-king ŭl ha-go ship-ŭn-de-yo.

I'd like to do (= use) valet parking/services.

08 투숙객 입니다.
tu-suk-gaek ip-ni-da.

I'm a staying guest.

09 체크인을 하려고 합니다.
che-kŭ-in-ŭl ha-ryŏ-go hap-ni-da.

I'd like to check in.

10 예약을 했어요.
ye-yag ŭl hae-ssŏ-yo.

I made a reservation.

11 예약 번호를 알려주시겠어요?
ye-yak bŏn-ho rŭl al-lyŏ-ju-shi-get-ssŏ-yo?

Could you tell me the reservation number?

12 예약 번호는 12345입니다.
ye-yak bŏn-ho nŭn il-i-sam-sa-o ip-ni-da.

The reservation number is 12345.

13 예약 번호가 생각이 안나네요.
ye-yak bŏn-ho ga saeng-gag i an-na-ne-yo.

I can't remember the reservation number.

14 대신, 이름을 알려드려도될까요?
dae-shin, i-rŭm ŭl al-lyŏ-dŭ-ryŏ-do doel-gga-yo?

Can I tell you (my) name instead?

15 여권을 보여주세요.
yŏ-ggwon ŭl bo-yŏ-ju-se-yo.

Please show me (your) passport.

16 신용카드가 필요합니다.
shin-yong-ka-dŭ ga pil-yo-hap-ni-da.

I need (your) credit card.

17 예치금을 내야 합니다.
ye-chi-gŭm ŭl nae-ya hap-ni-da.

(Lit) You have to pay a deposit.

18 현금으로 계산할게요.
hyŏn-gŭm ŭ-ro gye-san hal-gge-yo.

I will pay (with) cash.

19 체크아웃 할 때 신용카드로 낼게요.
che-kŭ-a-ut hal ttae shin-yong-ka-dŭ ro nael-gge-yo.

I'll pay with a credit card when I check-out.

20 짐이 많아요.
jim i man-a-yo.

I have a lot of luggage.

21 예약이 확인되지 않습니다.
ye-yag i hwag-in doe-ji an-sŭp-ni-da.

(Your) reservation can't be confirmed.
= I can't find your reservation.

22 예약이 없나요?
ye-yag i ŏp-na-yo?

You don't have (my) reservation?

23 다른 이름으로 찾아봐주세요.
da-rŭn i-rŭm ŭ-ro cha-ja-bwa-ju-se-yo.

Could you please look it up by/with a different name?

24 어느 날짜로 예약하셨죠?
ŏ-nŭ nal-jja ro ye-yak ha-shŏt-jyo?

What date did you make the reservation for?

25 여행사를 통해서 예약하셨나요?
yŏ-haeng-sa rŭl tong-hae-sŏ ye-yak ha-shŏt-na-yo?

Did you make the reservation through a travel agency?

26 예약하신 신용카드를 주세요.
ye-yak-ha-shin shin-yong-ka-dŭ rŭl ju-se-yo.

Please give me the credit card (you) made the reservation with?

27 인터넷으로 예약하셨나요?
in-tŏ-ne sŭ-ro ye-yak ha-shŏt-na-yo?

Did you make the reservation through the Internet?

28 멤버쉽이 있으신가요?
mem-bŏ-shib i i-ssŭ-shin-ga-yo?

Do you have a membership?

29 멤버쉽 카드 여기 있습니다.
mem-bŏ-ship ka-dŭ yŏ-gi it-ssŭp-ni-da.

Here is the membership card.

30 업그레이드 가능한가요?
ŏp-gŭ-re-i-dŭ ga-nŭng-han-ga-yo?

Is an upgrade possible?

31 오늘은 만실입니다.
o-nŭl ŭn man-shil ip-ni-da.

It's a full house today.

= We're fully booked today.

32 업그레이드 가능합니다.
ŏp-gŭ-re-i-dŭ ga-nŭng-hap-ni-da.

An upgrade is possible.

33 체크아웃은 몇시인가요?
che-kŭ-a-u sŭn myŏ-sshi in-ga-yo?

What time is check-out?

34 조금 늦게 체크아웃 해도 되나요?
jo-gŭm nŭt-ge che-kŭ-a-ut hae-do doe-na-yo?

Can I check-out a little late?

35 몇시까지 체크아웃 할 수 있나요?
myŏ-sshi gga-ji che-kŭ-a-ut hal su it-na-yo?

(Lit) Until what time can I check-out?

= What's the latest I can check-out?

36 두명이 투숙합니다.
du-myŏng i tu-suk-hap-ni-da.
2 person/people is/are/will be staying.

37 한명 더 투숙합니다.
han-myŏng dŏ tu-suk-hap-ni-da.
1 more person/people is/are/will be staying.

38 추가 요금이 있나요?
chu-ga yo-gŭm i it-na-yo?
Is there an additional charge?

39 추가 요금이 있습니다.
chu-ga yo-gŭm i it-ssŭp-ni-da.
There is an additional charge.

40 엘레베이터는 어디인가요?
el-le-be-i-tŏ nŭn ŏ-di-in-ga-yo?
Where is the elevator?

41 방까지 어떻게 가죠?
bang gga-ji ŏ-ttŏ-ke ga-jyo?
How do I get to the room?

42 짐을 먼저 방에 넣어 주세요.
jim ŭl mŏn-jŏ bang e nŏ-ŏ ju-se-yo.
Please put the luggage in the room first.

43 팁은 받지 않습니다.
tib ŭn bat-ji an-ssŭp-ni-da.
We don't accept tips.

44 예약을 하고 싶습니다.
ye-yag ŭl ha-go ship-sŭp-ni-da.
I'd like to make a reservation.

45 싱글/더블 베드로 주세요.
sing-gŭl/dŏ-bŭl be-dŭ ro hae ju-se-yo.
Give me a single/double bed, please.

46 아이가 있습니다.
a-i ga it-ssŭp-ni-da.
I have a child.

47 몇 명이세요?
myŏt myŏng i-se-yo?
How many people is it?

48 한명/두명/세명 입니다.
han-myŏng/du-myŏng/se-myŏng ip-ni-da.
It's 1/2/3 person/people.

49 연결된 방이 있나요?
yŏn-gyŏl-doen bang i it-na-yo?
Do you have connecting/adjoining rooms?

50 뷰가 좋은 방을 부탁드립니다.
byu ga jo-ŭn bang ŭl bu-tak-dŭ-rip-ni-da.

Please give me a room (with) a nice view.

51 주차장은 어디죠?
ju-cha-jang ŭn ŏ-di-jyo?

Where is the parking lot?

52 얼마나 머무실 예정이세요?
ŏl-ma-na mŏ-mu-shil ye-jŏng-i-se-yo?

(Lit) How long is your plan on staying?

= How long do you plan to stay?

53 2박 3일이요.
i-bak sam-il i-yo.

It's 3 days and 2 nights.

54 예치금이 얼마죠?
ye-chi-gŭm i ŏl-ma-jyo?

How much is the deposit?

55 어떻게 결제하시겠어요?
ŏ-ttŏ-ke gyŏl-je ha-shi-get-ssŏ-yo?

How would you like to make a payment?

56 체크인은 몇시죠?
che-kŭ-in ŭn myŏ-sshi-jyo?

What time is check in?

57 방이 아직 준비되지 않았습니다.
bang i a-jik jun-bi doe-ji an-a-ssŭp-ni-da.

The room isn't ready yet.

58 방이 준비되면 연락주세요.
bang i jun-bi doe-myŏn yŏl-lak-ju-se-yo.

Please call me when the room is ready.

59 방이 준비되었습니다.
bang i jun-bi doe-ŏ-ssŭp-ni-da.

The room is ready.

60 여기 룸키입니다.
yŏ-gi rum-ki ip-ni-da.

Here is the room key.

61 룸키 하나 더 주세요.
rum-ki ha-na dŏ ju-se-yo.

Give me one more room key, please.

62 방 번호는 100 입니다.
bang bŏn-ho nŭn baek ip-ni-da.

The room number 100.

63 제 방은 몇 층인가요?
je bang ŭn myŏt chŭng in-ga-yo?

What floor is my room?

64 방까지 안내 해주세요.
bang gga-ji an-nae hae-ju-se-yo.

Please guide me to the room.

65 짐을 여기에 맡겨도 되나요?
jim-ŭl yŏ-gi e mat-gyŏ-do doe-na-yo?

May I leave (my) baggage (at) here?

66 성이 어떻게 되시죠?
sŏng i ŏ-ttŏ-ke doe-shi-jyo?

What is (your) last name?

67 성함 스펠링을 알려주세요.
sŏng-ham sŭ-pel-ling ŭl al-lyŏ-ju-se-yo.

(Lit) Could you tell me
the spelling (of your) name?

68 체크아웃 하겠습니다.
che-kŭ-a-ut ha-get-ssŭp-ni-da.

I'm going to check-out.

69 불편한 건 없으셨나요?
bul-pyŏn-han gŏn ŏp-ssŭ-shŏt-na-yo?

(Lit) Wasn't there anything uncomfortable?
= Was everything fine with your stay?

70 편안한 숙박 되셨나요?
pyŏn-an-han suk-bak doe-shŏt-na-yo?

(Lit) Did it become a comfortable stay?
= Was everything all right with your stay?

71 방에 지갑을/여권을 놓고 왔어요.
bang e ji-gab ŭl/yŏ-ggwŏn ŭl no-ko wa-ssŏ-yo.

I left (my) wallet/passport in the room.

72 룸서비스 입니다.
rum-sŏ-bi-sŭ ip-ni-da.

It's room service.

73 식사를 주문하고 싶은데요.
shik-sa rŭl ju-mun ha-go ship-ŭn-de-yo.

I'd like to order a meal.

74 몇시까지 주문 가능한가요?
myŏ-sshi gga-ji ju-mun ga-nŭng-han-ga-yo?

(Lit) Until what time can I order?
= What's the latest I can order?

75 룸 차지로 해주세요.
rum cha-ji ro hae-ju-se-yo.

(Lit) Make it (as) a room charge, please.
= Charge the room, please.

76 서명 부탁드립니다.
sŏ-myŏng bu-tak-dŭ-rip-ni-da.

May I get (Your) signature, please.

77 얼음을 더 갖다주세요.
ŏl-ŭm ŭl dŏ gat-da-ju-se-yo.

Bring me more ice, please.

78 얼음은 어디에 있나요?
ŏl-ŭm ŭn ŏ-di e it-na-yo?
(At) where is ice?

79 부엌이 있나요?
bu-ŏk i it-na-yo?
Is there a kitchen?

80 취사해도 되나요?
chwi-sa hae-do doe-na-yo?
May I cook?

81 지배인을 불러주세요.
ji-bae-in ŭl bul-lŏ-ju-se-yo.
Call (= get) me the manager, please.

82 시트를 교체해 주세요.
shi-tŭ rŭl gyo-che hae ju-se-yo.
Please change the sheets.

83 방 청소를 해 주세요.
bang chŏng-so rŭl hae-ju-se-yo.
(Lit) Please clean up (my) room.
= Please make up (my) room.

84 청소가 안 되어 있어요.
chŏng-so ga an doe-ŏ i-ssŏ-yo.
It has not been cleaned/made up.

85 예약을 안 했는데, 방 있나요?
ye-yag ŭl an haet-nŭn-de, bang it-na-yo?
I did not make a reservation, but do you have a room?

86 더 저렴한 방은 없나요?
dŏ jŏ-ryŏm-han bang ŭn ŏp-na-yo?
Don't you have a more cheap (= cheaper) room?

87 방을 볼 수 있나요?
bang ŭl bol su it-na-yo?
May I see the room?

88 조식이 포함되어 있나요?
jo-shig i po-ham doe-ŏ it-na-yo?
Is breakfast included?

89 에어컨이 고장 났습니다.
e-ŏ-kŏn i go-jang na-ssŭp-ni-da.
(Lit) A/C is out of order.
= A/C isn't working.

90 베개가 없습니다.
be-gae ga ŏp-ssŭp-ni-da.
There is no pillow.

91 더운 물이 안 나와요.
dŏ-un mul i an na-wa-yo.
(Lit) Hot water is not coming out.
= There is no hot water.

92

7시에 깨워주세요.
il-gop shi e ggae-wŏ-ju-se-yo.

Please wake me up at 7 o'clock.

93

짐을 잠시 보관 해주세요.
jim ŭl jam-shi bo-gwan hae-ju-se-yo.

Please hold (my) luggage for a while.

94

룸키를 잃어버렸어요.
rum-ki rŭl il-ŏ-bŏ-ryŏ-ssŏ-yo.

I lost (my) room key.

95

시내 지도 있나요?
shi-nae ji-do it-na-yo?

Do you have a map (of) the city?

96

하루 더 있겠습니다.
ha-ru dŏ it-get-ssŭp-ni-da.

I'd like to be here (= stay) one more day.

97

하루 더 묵을 수 있나요?
ha-ru dŏ mug-ŭl su it-na-yo?

Can I stay one more day?

98

택시를 불러 주세요.
tek-shi rŭl bul-lŏ ju-se-yo.

Please call a taxi for me.

Chapter 12. DIRECTIONS

01 길을 잃었어요.
gil ŭl il-ŏ-ssŏ-yo.

(Lit) I've lost direction. = I'm lost.

02 길을 잃은 것 같아요.
gil ŭl il-ŭn gŏt gat-a-yo.

(Lit) I think I've lost direction.

= I think I'm lost.

03 여기가 어디죠?
yŏ-gi ga ŏ-di-jyo?

(Lit) Where is here? = Where am I?

04 제가 지금 어디에 있죠?
je ga ji-gŭm ŏ-di e it-jyo?

(At) where am I now?

05 실례합니다. 길 좀 여쭤볼게요.
shil-lye-hap-ni-da. gil jom yŏ-jjwŏ-bol-gge-yo.

(Lit) Pardon me, let me ask you for some directions.

06 길 좀 알려주시겠어요?
gil jom al-lyŏ-ju-shi-get-ssŏ-yo?

(Lit) Could you please tell me the directions?

07 홍대까지 어떻게 가나요?
hong-dae gga-ji ŏ-ttŏ-ke ga-na-yo?

How do I get to Hongdae?

08 거리 이름이 뭐죠?
gŏ-ri i-rŭm i mwŏ-jyo?

What's the name (of) the street?

09 이/저 빌딩 이름이 뭐죠?
i / jŏ bil-ding i-rŭm i mwŏ-jyo?

What's the name (of) this/that building?

10 걸어서 갈 수 있나요?
gŏl-ŏ-sŏ gal su it-na-yo?

Can I go on foot (walking)?

= Is it within walking distance?

11 걸어서 얼마나 걸릴까요?
gŏl-ŏ-sŏ ŏl-ma-na gŏl-lil-gga-yo?

How long would it take by walking?

12 20분/한시간 정도 걸립니다.
i-ship bun/han shi-gan jŏng-do gŏl-lip-ni-da.

It takes about 20 minutes / 1 hour(s).

13 걸어서 가기에는 너무 멀어요.
gŏl-ŏ-sŏ ga-gi-e nŭn nŏ-mu mŏl-ŏ-yo.

(Lit) It's too far to go by walking.

= It's too far to walk there.

14 가까운 거리예요.
ga-gga-un gŏ-ri ye-yo.

It's a close/near distance.

15 아주 가까워요/멀어요.
a-ju ga-gga-wŏ-yo / mŏl-ŏ-yo.

(It's) very close/far (from here).

16 직진하세요.
jik-jin ha-se-yo.

(Lit) Do a going straight.

= Go straight.

17 이쪽으로 쭉 가세요.
i jjok ŭ-ro jjuk ga-se-yo.

Keep going (to) this way.

18 이 방향으로 계속 가세요.
i bang-hyang ŭ-ro gye-sok ga-se-yo.

Continue going (to) this direction.

19 이쪽으로/저쪽으로 가야 하나요?
i jjog ŭ-ro / jŏ jjog ŭ-ro ga-ya ha-na-yo?

Should I go (to) this way/that way?

20 세블럭 후 왼쪽/오른쪽입니다.
se-bŭl-lŏk hu oen-jjog/o-rŭn-jjog ip-ni-da.

After 3 blocks, it's (on) the left/right.

21 지하철 말고 다른 방법은 없나요?
ji-ha-chŏl mal-go da-rŭn bang-bŏb ŭn ŏp-na-yo?

Isn't there another way besides the subway?

22 근처에 화장실이 있나요?
gŭn-chŏ-e hwa-jang-shil i it-na-yo?

Is there a restroom nearby?

23 홍대가는 법 좀 알려주세요.
hong-dae ga-nŭn bŏp jom al-lyŏ-ju-se-yo.

Please tell me how to get (to) Hongdae.

24 홍대까지 가는 길을 알고 싶어요.
hong-dae gga-ji ga-nŭn gil ŭl al-go ship-ŏ-yo.

I'd like to know the directions to get to Hongdae.

25 왼쪽으로/오른쪽으로 가세요.
oen-jjog ŭ-ro/o-rŭn-jjog ŭ-ro ga-se-yo.

Go (to) left/right.

26 이쪽입니다/저쪽입니다.
i jjog ip-ni-da / jŏ jjog ip-ni-da.

It's this way/that way.

27 바로 근처예요.
ba-ro gŭn-chŏ-ye-yo.

It's right nearby.

28 여기/저기 있네요.
yŏ-gi / jŏ-gi it-ne-yo.

Here/There it is.

29 길을 따라 내려가세요.
gil ŭl tta-ra nae-ryŏ-ga-se-yo.

Go down along the road.

30 우체국 지나서 있어요.
u-che-gug ji-na-sŏ i-ssŏ-yo.

It's past the post office.

31 도와주셔서 감사합니다.
do-wa-ju-shŏ-sŏ gam-sa-hap-ni-da.

Thanks for helping (me).
/ I appreciate your help.

32 첫째/둘째 골목으로 들어가세요.
chŏt-jjae/dul-jjae gol-mog ŭ-ro dŭl-ŏ-ga-se-yo.

Go into the first/second alley.

33 우체국 맞은편에 있어요.
u-che-guk ma-zŭn-pyŏn e i-ssŏ-yo.

It's across from the post office.

34 우체국 바로 뒤에 있어요.
u-che-guk ba-ro dwi-e i-ssŏ-yo.

It's right behind the post office.

35 우체국 바로 옆에 있어요.
u-che-guk ba-ro yŏp-e i-ssŏ-yo.

It's right next to the post office.

36 세모 빌딩 3층입니다.
se-mo bil-ding sam chŭng ip-ni-da.

(Lit) It's floor 3, Semo building.

37 저도 모르겠어요.
jŏ do mo-rŭ-get-ssŏ-yo.
I don't know, either.

38 저 분/이 분에게 물어보세요.
jŏ bun / i bun e-ge mul-ŏ-bo-se-yo.
Ask (to) that/this gentleman/lady.

39 정확하지는 않아요.
jŏng-hwak-ha-ji-nŭn an-a-yo.
It's not accurate/exact.

40 저도 그 방향으로 갑니다.
jŏ do gŭ bang-hyang ŭ-ro gap-ni-da.
I'm going (to) that way/direction too.

41 혹시 이 주소를 아시나요?
hok-shi i ju-so rŭl a-shi-na-yo?
Do you know this address, by any chance?

42 혹시 이 건물이 어디있는지 아시나요?
hok-shi i gŏn-mul i ŏ-di-in-nŭn-ji a-shi-na-yo?
Do you know where this building is, by any chance?

43 제가 맞게 찾아왔나요?
je ga mat-ge cha-ja-wat-na-yo?
(Lit) Did I come correctly?
= Did I come to the right place?

44 초행이라 잘 모르겠어요.
cho-haeng i-ra jal mo-rŭ-get-ssŏ-yo.
I'm not quite sure because it's my first time (coming here).

45 제가 안내해 드릴게요.
je ga an-nae hae dŭ-ril-gge-yo.
I will guide you.

46 바로 찾으실 거예요.
ba-ro cha-zŭ-shil gŏ-ye-yo.
(Lit) You will find it immediately.
= You can't miss it.

47 A와 B사이에 있습니다.
A-wa B-sa-i-e it-ssŭp-ni-da.
It's between A and B.

48 저를 따라오세요.
jŏ rŭl tta-ra-o-se-yo.
Please follow me.

49 한번 더 설명 해주세요.
han-bŏn dŏ sŏl-myŏng hae-ju-se-yo.
Please explain it to me one more time.

50 병원을 찾고 있습니다.
byŏng-wŏn ŭl chat-go it-ssŭp-ni-da.
I'm looking for a hospital.

51 약도를 그려 주시겠어요?
yak-do rŭl gŭ-ryŏ ju-shi-get-ssŏ-yo?

Could you draw a rough map, please?

52 이 지도에서 현재 위치가 어디인가요?
i ji-do-e-sŏ hyŏn-jae wi-chi ga
ŏ-di-in-ga-yo?

Where is the current location from this map?

53 블록을 끼고 우회전/좌회전 하세요.
bŭl-log ŭl ggi-go u-hoe-jŏn / jwa-hoe-jŏn ha-se-yo.

Turn right/left onto the block.

54 약도를 그려드릴게요.
yak-do rŭl gŭ-ryŏ dŭ-ril-gge-yo.

I will draw a rough map for you.

55 방금 지나친 것 같아요.
bang-gŭm ji-na-chin gŏt gat-a-yo.

I think we just passed it.

56 조금 더 가야해요.
jo-gŭm dŏ ga-ya-hae-yo.

We need to go a little more.

57 여기 지리를 잘 아시나요?
yŏ-gi ji-ri rŭl jal a-shi-na-yo?

(Lit) Do you know the geography here well?

= Are you familiar with this area?

58 지름길이 있나요?
ji-rŭm-gil i it-na-yo?

Is there a shortcut?

59 어느 쪽 인가요?
ŏ-nŭ jjok in-ga-yo?

Which way is it?

Chapter 13. HEALTH & HOSPITAL & PHARMACY

01 건강은 어떠세요?
gŏn-gang ŭn jom ŏ-ttŏ-se-yo?

(Lit) How is (your) health?

= How are you feeling?

02 몸은 나아졌어요?
mom ŭn na-a-jyŏ-ssŏ-yo?

(Lit) Is (your) body better?

= Are you feeling better?

03 건강이 별로 안 좋아요.
gŏn-gang i byŏl-lo an jo-a-yo.

(Lit) (My) health is not very good.

= I'm not feeling well.

04 몸이 안 좋아요.
mom i an-jo-a-yo.

(Lit) (My) body is not well.

= I'm not feeling well.

05 컨디션이 좋아요.
kŏn-di-shŏn i jo-a-yo.

(Lit) (My) condition is good.

= I'm doing well.

06 별로 아프지 않아요.
byŏl-lo a-pŭ-ji an-a-yo.

(Lit) It doesn't hurt that much.

= I'm not that sick.

07 잘 아프지 않아요.
jal a-pŭ-ji an-a-yo.

(Lit) I'm not sick easily.

I rarely get sick

08 아파서 누워 있어요.
a-pa-sŏ nu-wŏ-i-ssŏ-yo.

I'm lying (in bed) because I'm sick.

09 몸이 다 아파요.
mom i da a-pa-yo.

(I) ache all over (my) body.

10 배가 아파요.
bae ga a-pa-yo.

(Lit) (My) stomach hurts.

= I have a stomach ach.

11 열이 있어요.
yŏl i i-ssŏ-yo.

I have a fever.

= I'm running a fever.

12 생리통이 있어요.
saeng-ni-tong i i-ssŏ-yo.

I'm having menstrual pain.

13 독감이 유행이에요.
dok-gam i yu-haeng-i-e-yo.

(Lit) The flu is popular.

= There's a flu going around.

14 감기 조심하세요.
gam-gi jo-shim-ha-se-yo.

(Lit) Be careful with a cold.

= Be careful not to catch a cold.

15 감기 걸린 것 같아요.
gam-gi gŏl-lin gŏt gat-a-yo.

(Lit) I think I caught a cold.

= I think I'm coming down with a cold.

16 감기든 목소리네요.
gam-gi-dŭn mok-so-ri ne-yo.

(Lit) (Your) voice is cold-struck.

You sound like you've got a cold.

17 기침을 많이 해요.
gi-chim ŭl man-i hae-yo.

(Lit) I do cough a lot.

18 머리가 아파요.
mŏ-ri ga a-pa-yo.

(Lit) (My) head hurts.

= I have a headache.

19 콧물이 나요.
kot-mul i na-yo.

(Lit) Nose water (= nasal discharge) is coming out.

I have a runny nose.

20 팔이/다리가 부러졌어요.
pal i / da-ri ga bu-rŏ-jyŏ-ssŏ-yo.

(My) arm/leg is broken.

21 여드름이 났어요.
yŏ-dŭ-rŭm i na-ssŏ-yo.

(Lit) Acne has grown.

= I have acne.

22 부상당했어요.
bu-sang dang-hae-ssŏ-yo.

I'm injured.

23 온몸이 멍 들었어요.
on mom i mŏng dŭl-ŏ-ssŏ-yo.

I'm bruised all over (my) body.

24 다 나았어요.
da na-a-ssŏ-yo.

I'm all better now. / I'm not sick anymore.

25 하나도 안 아파요.
ha-na-do an a-pa-yo.

I'm not sick/hurt at all.

26 갈비뼈가 부러졌어요.
gal-bi-bbyŏ ga bu-rŏ-jyŏ-ssŏ-yo.

(Lit) (My) rib is fractured.

= I fractured a rib.

27 넘어졌어요.
nŏm-ŏ-jyŏ-ssŏ-yo.

I fell down.

28 미끄러졌어요.
mi-ggŭ-rŏ-jyŏ-ssŏ-yo.

I slipped (and fell).

29 완전히 지쳤어요.
wan-jŏn-hi ji-chyŏ-ssŏ-yo.

I'm completely exhausted.

30 건강해 보여요!
gŏn-gang-hae bo-yŏ-yo!

You look healthy!

31 안색이 안 좋아보여요.
an-saeg i an jo-a-bo-yŏ-yo.

(Lit) (Your) complexion doesn't look good.

32 발진이 났어요.
bal-jin i na-ssŏ-yo.

(Lit) A rash has grown.

= I have a rash.

33 목이 뻐근해요.
mog i bbŏ-gŭn-hae-yo.

(My) neck is stiff.

34 계속 재채기가 나요.
gye-sok jae-chae-gi ga na-yo.

(Lit) Cough keeps coming out.

= I can't stop sneezing.

35 입술이 텄어요.
ip-sul i tŏ-ssŏ-yo.

(My) lips are chapped.

36 좋아지고 있어요.
jo-a-ji-go i-ssŏ-yo.

(I'm) getting better.

37 좀 쉬세요.
jom shwi-se-yo.

Rest a little.

38 과로하지 마세요!
gwa-ro ha-ji ma-se-yo!

(Lit) Don't work too much!

= Don't overdo yourself.

39 병원에 가보세요.
byŏng-wŏn e ga-bo-se-yo.

You should go to a hospital.

40 그 정도는 아니에요.
gŭ jŏng-do nŭn a-ni-e-yo.

(Lit) It's not to such an extent.

= It's not that bad.

41 몸조리 잘 하세요.
mom-jo-ri jal ha-se-yo.

(Lit) Do a good job (of) taking care of yourself.

Take good care of yourself.

42 쾌유를 빕니다.
kwae-yu rŭl bip-ni-da.

Hope your full recovery.

43 너무 피곤해요.
nŏ-mu pi-gon-hae-yo.

I'm too tired.

AT THE HOSPITAL

01 근처에 병원이 있나요?
gŭn-chŏ-e byŏng-wŏn i it-na-yo?

Is there a hospital nearby?

02 병원에 좀 데려다 주세요.
byŏng-wŏn e jom de-ryŏ-da ju-se-yo.

Please take me to a hospital.

03 제가 병원에 데려다 드릴게요.
je ga byŏng-wŏn e de-ryŏ-da dŭ-ril-gge-yo.

I will take you to a hospital.

04 구급차를 불러주세요.
gu-gŭp-cha rŭl bul-lŏ ju-se-yo.

Please call an ambulance.

05 의사를 불러주세요.
ŭi-sa rŭl bul-lŏ ju-se-yo.

Please call a doctor.

06 응급상황입니다.
ŭng-gŭp sang-hwang ip-ni-da.

It's an urgent situation.
= It's an emergency.

07 안색이 좋지 않아요.
an-saeg i jot-chi an-a-yo.

(Lit) (Your) complexion isn't good.

You aren't looking very well.

08 몸에 기운이 하나도 없습니다.
mom e gi-un i ha-na-do ŏp-sŭp-ni-da.

(Lit) I don't have energy in (my) body at all.

I feel so weak.

09 어디가 아파서 오셨나요?
ŏ-di ga a-pa-sŏ o-shŏt-na-yo?

(Lit) What pain made you come here?

= What brought you here?

10 환자분 성함이 어떻게 되세요?
hwan-ja-bun sŏng-ham i ŏ-ttŏ-ke doe-se-yo?

What's the name (of) the patient?

11 의료보험이 있나요?
ŭi-ryo bo-hŏm i it-na-yo?

Do you have medical insurance?

12 접수를 도와드리겠습니다.
jŏp-su rŭl do-wa-dŭ-ri-get-sŭp-ni-da.

I will help you with registration.

13 의사선생님이 곧 오실거예요.
ŭi-sa-sŏn-saeng-nim i got o-shil-gŏ-ye-yo.

The doctor will come soon.

14 복용중인 약이 있나요?
bog-yong jung-in yag i it-na-yo?

(Lit) Is there a medicine you are taking?

Are you taking any medications?

15 알러지가 있나요?
al-lŏ-ji ga it-na-yo?

Do you have (any) allergies?

16 지병이 있나요?
ji-byŏng i it-na-yo?

Do you have (any)
pre-existing conditions (diseases)?

17 입을 벌려보세요.
ib ŭl bŏl-lyŏ-bo-se-yo.

Open (your) mouth, please.

18 아 해보세요.
a hae-bo-se-yo.

(Lit) Do an "Ah"

Say "Ah".

19 숨을 크게 쉬어보세요.
sum ŭl kŭ-ge shwi-ŏ-bo-se-yo.

(Lit) Try breathing a big breath.

Take a deep breath.

20 체온을 재볼게요.
che-on ŭl jae-bol-gge-yo.

I will measure (your) body temperature.

21 주사를 맞아야 겠습니다.
ju-sa rŭl ma-ja-ya get-sŭp-ni-da.

You need to get a shot (injection).

22 주사를 놔드릴게요.
ju-sa rŭl nwa-dŭ-ril-gge-yo.

I will inject (= give) you a shot.

23 조금 따끔합니다.
jo-gŭm tta-ggŭm-hap-ni-da.

It stings a little.

24 지혈해드릴게요.
ji-hyŏl hae-dŭ-ril-gge-yo.

I will make it stop bleeding.

25 피가 계속 나요.
pi ga gye-sok na-yo.

(Lit) Blood keeps coming out.

I keep bleeding.

26 열이 많이 나네요.
yŏl i man-i na-ne-yo.

(You) have a lot of fever.

= You're running a high fever.

27 더 큰 병원으로 가야 합니다.
dŏ kŭn byŏng-wŏn ŭ-ro ga-ya hap-ni-da.

You must go to a bigger hospital.

28 심각한 상황입니다.
shim-gak-han sang-hwang ip-ni-da.

It's a serious situation.

29 엑스레이를 찍어봅시다.
ek-sŭ-re-i rŭl jjig-ŏ bop-shi-da.

Let's take an x-ray.

30 수술을 해야합니다.
su-sul ŭl hae-ya-hap-ni-da.

You need to have surgery.

31 왜 이렇게 늦게 오셨어요?
wae i-rŏt-ke nŭt-gge o-shŏ-ssŏ-yo?

Why did you come this late?

32 큰 일 날 뻔 했습니다.
kŭn il nal bbŏn haet-ssŭp-ni-da.

(Lit) It could have been a huge ordeal.

= It could have been so much worse.

33 처방전을 드리겠습니다.
chŏ-bang-jŏn ŭl dŭ-ri-get-sŭp-ni-da.

I will give you a prescription.

34 약국에서 약을 받아가세요.
yak-gug e-sŏ yag ŭl bad-a-ga-se-yo.

Pick up (your) medications from the pharmacy.

35 상태를 자세히 관찰하세요.
sang-tae rŭl ja-se-hi gwan-chal-ha-se-yo.

Monitor (your) condition carefully.

36 약을 잊지말고 드세요.
yag ŭl it-ji-mal-go dŭ-se-yo.

Don't forget to eat (= take) the meds.

37 병원에 또 와야하나요?
byŏng-wŏn e tto wa-ya ha-na-yo?

Do I have to come to the hospital

(= doctor's office) again?

38 아니요, 이제 안 오셔도 됩니다.
a-ni-yo, i-je an o-shŏ-do doep-ni-da.

(Lit) No, not coming is okay now.

No, you don't have to come anymore.

39 입원 하셔야 합니다.
ib-wŏn ha-shŏ-ya hap-ni-da.

You need to be hospitalized.

= You need to stay in the hospital

40 퇴원 하셔도 됩니다.
toe-wŏn ha-shŏ-do doep-ni-da.

(Lit) You can get discharged from the hospital.

= You may go home now.

41 피검사를 해보는게 좋겠습니다.
pi gŏm-sa rŭl hae-bo-nŭn-ge jo-ket-sŭp-ni-da.

I think it's better to run a blood test.

42 다른 불편한 곳은 없으신가요?
da-rŭn bul-pyŏn-han go sŭn ŏp-sŭ-shin-ga-yo?

(Lit) Isn't there another uncomfortable spot?

Is there anything else that's bothering you?

43 어떤 증상이 있죠?
ŏ-ttŏn jŭng-sang i it-jyo?

What kind of symptoms do you have?

93

44 혀를 내밀어 보세요.
hyŏ rŭl nae-mil-ŏ bo-se-yo.

Try sticking out (your) tongue.

45 침대에 누워계세요.
chim-dae e nu-wŏ-gye-se-yo.

Stay lying down on the bed.

46 그만 오셔도 될 것 같습니다.
gŭ-man o-shŏ-do doel gŏt gat-sŭp-ni-da.

(Lit) I think you can stop coming.

= You don't need to come back anymore.

47 물을 많이 드세요.
mul ŭl man-i dŭ-se-yo.

Eat (= drink) a lot of water.

48 혈압을 재보겠습니다.
hyŏl-ab ŭl jae-bo-get-sŭp-ni-da.

I will measure (your) blood pressure.

49 혈압이 높군요.
hyŏl-ab i nop-gun-nyo.

(Lit) (Your) blood pressure is high.

50 정상입니다.
jŏng-sang ip-ni-da.

It's normal.

51 눈물이 납니다.
nun-mul i nap-ni-da.

(Lit) Tears come out.

I have teary eyes.

52 눈이 너무 건조해요.
nun i nŏ-mu gŏn-jo-hae-yo.

My eyes are too dry.

53 어지럽습니다.
ŏ-ji-rŏp-sŭp-ni-da.

I feel dizzy.

54 약을 복용 중입니다.
yag ŭl bog-yong jung-ip-ni-da.

(Lit) I'm taking medicines (now).

I'm on medication now.

55 약을 복용하고 있나요?
yag ŭl bog-yong ha-go it-na-yo?

(Lit) Are you taking (your) medicine?

= Have you been taking your medications?

56 발목을 삐었어요.
bal-mog ŭl bbi-ŏ-ssŏ-yo.

I sprained (my) ankle.

AT THE PHARMACY

01 이 약을 주세요.
i yag ŭl ju-se-yo.

Please give me this medicine.

02 처방전을 주세요.
chŏ-bang-jŏn-ŭl ju-se-yo.

Please give me the prescription.

03 처방전이 있어야 하나요?
chŏ-bang-jŏn i i-ssŏ-ya ha-na-yo?

Do I need to have a prescription?

04 처방전 없이 살 수 있나요?
chŏ-bang-jŏn ŏp-shi sal su it-na-yo?

Can I buy (it) without a prescription?

05 이게 무슨 약이죠?
i-ge mu-sŭn yag i-jyo?

What medicine is this?

06 의사 소견서를 주세요.
ŭi-sa so-gyŏn-sŏ rŭl ju-se-yo.

Please give me the doctor's note.

07 처방약 나왔습니다.
chŏ-bang-yak na-wa-ssŭp-ni-da.

(Lit) The prescribed medicine came out.

= Here's your prescribed medicine.

08 하루에 몇 번 먹어야 하나요?
ha-ru-e myŏt bŏn mŏg-ŏ-ya ha-na-yo?

How many times do I have to eat

(= take) it a day?

09 하루에 세 번, 식 후 30분이요.
ha-ru-e se bŏn, shik hu sam-ship bun-i-yo.

Three times a day,

30 minutes after a meal.

10 규칙적으로 약을 복용하세요.
gyu-chik-jŏg-ŭ-ro yag ŭl bog-yong ha-se-yo.

Take (your) medicine regularly.

11 한 번에 한 알 이상 드시면 안돼요.
han bŏn-e han al i-sang dŭ-shi-myŏn an-doe-yo.

You shouldn't eat (= take)
more than one pill at a time.

12 깊이 베인데 바를 것 있나요?
gip-i be-in-de ba-rŭl gŏt it-na-yo?

(Lit) Is there anything to apply on
where cut deeply?

13 이 연고를 상처에 바르세요.
i yŏn-go rŭl sang-chŏ-e ba-rŭ-se-yo.

Apply this cream/ointment on the cut.

14 1회용 밴드를 붙이세요.
il-hoe-yong baen-dŭ rŭl bu-chi-se-yo.

(Lit) Attach (= put) (this) one-time-use band.

15 부작용은 없을까요?
bu-jag-yong ŭn ŏp-ssŭl-gga-yo?

(Lit) Won't there be side effects?

16 제가 아는 바로는 없습니다.
je ga a-nŭn ba-ro nŭn ŏp-ssŭp-ni-da.

As far as I know, there isn't.

17 이 약을 먹고 나면 졸릴 수 있어요.
i yag ŭl mŏk-go na-myŏn jol-lil su do i-ssŏ-yo.

You might get sleepy after eating (= taking) this medicine.

18 낮에는 복용하지 마세요.
na-je nŭn bo-gyong ha-ji ma-se-yo.

Do not take it in the daytime.

19 증상이 계속되면 병원으로 가세요.
jŭng-sang i gye-sok-doe-myŏn byŏng-wŏn ŭ-ro ga-se-yo.

If the symptoms persist, go to a hospital.

20 처방전 없이는 약을 드릴 수 없습니다.
chŏ-bang-jŏn ŏp-shi nŭn yag ŭl dŭ-ril su ŏp-sŭp-ni-da.

I can't give you the medication without prescription.

21 그 증상에는 이 약이 잘 듣습니다.
gŭ jŭng-sang e nŭn i yag i jal dŭt-ssŭp-ni-da.

This medicine works well for that symptom.

22 효과가 있으면 좋겠네요.
hyo-ggwa ga i-ssŭ-myŏn jo-ket-ne-yo.

(Lit) It'd be nice if it has effectiveness.

= I hope this works.

23 이 약은 어디에 있나요?
i yag ŭn ŏ-di e it-na-yo?

(At) where is this medicine?

24 두 약의 차이점은 뭐죠?
du yag ŭi cha-i-jŏm ŭn mwŏ-jyo?

What's the difference (between) the two medicines?

25 뭐가 더 잘 듣나요?
mwŏ ga dŏ jal dŭt-na-yo?

(Lit) Which one works more well?

= Which one works better?

96

Chapter 14. TOURIST ATTRACTION

01 여기가 유명한 관광지 인가요?
yŏ-gi ga yu-myŏng-han gwan-gwang-ji in-ga-yo?
(Lit) Is here (= this) a famous tourist spot?

02 네, 아주 유명합니다.
ne, a-ju yu-myŏng-hap-ni-da.
Yes, it's very famous.

03 사람들이 굉장히 많네요.
sa-ram-dŭl i goeng-jang-hi man-ne-yo.
There are so many people.

04 관광객이 많습니다.
gwan-gwang-gaek i man-sŭp-ni-da.
There are a lot of tourists.

05 언제나 사람이 많아요.
ŏn-je-na sa-ram i man-a-yo.
There are always a lot of people.

06 평일에도 붐빕니다.
pyŏng-il e-do bum-bip-ni-da.
It's crowded even during the week.

07 인기가 많은 곳입니다.
in-gi-ga man-ŭn go ship-ni-da.
It's a popular place.

08 역사적인 곳입니다.
yŏ-k-sa-jŏg-in go ship-ni-da.
It's a historical place.

09 이 곳은 어떤 곳인가요?
i go sŭn ŏ-ttŏn go shin-ga-yo?
What kind of place is this?

10 어떠한 의미가 있나요?
ŏ-ttŏ-han ŭi-mi ga it-na-yo?

(Lit) What kind of meaning does it have?

11 영어 안내 책자가 있나요?
yŏng-ŏ an-nae chaek-ja ga it-na-yo?

Do you have an English guidebook?

12 영어 안내원이 있나요?
yŏng-ŏ an-nae-wŏn i it-na-yo?

Do you have an English guide?

13 오디오 가이드가 있나요?
o-di-o ga-i-dŭ ga it-na-yo?

Do you have an audio guide?

14 티켓은 어디서 사나요?
ti-ke sŭn ŏ-di-sŏ sa-na-yo?

(From) where do I buy the ticket?

15 화장실은 어디에 있나요?
hwa-jang-shil ŭn ŏ-di-e it-na-yo?

(At) where is the restroom?

16 입장 후에도 화장실이 있나요?
ip-jang hu-e do hwa-jang-shil i it-na-yo?

Is there a restroom after the entrance, too?

17 안내소는 어디인가요?
an-nae-so nŭn ŏ-di in-ga-yo?

Where is the information booth?

18 여권이 필요한가요?
yŏ-ggwŏn i pil-yo-han-ga-yo?

Is a passport necessary?

19 사진을 찍어도 되나요?
sa-jin ŭl jjig-ŏ-do doe-na-yo?

Can I take a picture?

20 사진 좀 찍어주시겠어요?
sa-jin jom jjig-ŏ ju-shi-get-ssŏ-yo?

Can you please take a picture for me?

21 사진 찍어드릴까요?
sa-jin jjig-ŏ dŭ-ril-gga-yo?

(Lit) Should I take a picture for you?

= Do you want me to take a picture for you?

22 배경이 나오게 찍어주세요.
bae-gyŏng i na-o-ge jjig-ŏ ju-se-yo.

(Lit) Please take (with) the background visible.

23 어른 한 장, 어린이 두 장 주세요.
ŏ-rŭn han jang, ŏ-rin-i du jang ju-se-yo.

Give me one ticket (for) adult, two tickets (for) kids.

24 몇시까지 입장해야 하나요?
myŏ-sshi gga-ji ip-jang hae-ya ha-na-yo?

By what time do I have to go in?

25 몇시까지 구경 가능한가요?
myŏ-sshi gga-ji gu-gyŏng ga-nŭng-han-ga-yo?

(Lit) Until what time can we look around?

What's the latest we can look around?

26 출구가 어디죠?
chul-gu ga ŏ-di-jyo?

Where is the exit?

27 동영상을 찍어도 되나요?
dong-yŏng-sang ŭl jjig-ŏ-do doe-na-yo?

Can I take a video?

28 입장 제한 구역입니다.
ip-jang je-han gu-yeog ip-ni-da.

(It's) a restricted (entrance) area.

29 왼쪽으로/오른쪽으로 걸으세요.
oen-jjog ŭ-ro / o-rŭn-jjog ŭ-ro gŏl-ŭ-se-yo.

(Lit) Walk on the left/right.

Keep left/right (when walking).

30 여기서 만나요.
yŏ-gi-sŏ man-na-yo.

(Lit) Let's meet at here.

31 입장료는 얼마죠?
ip-jang-nyo nŭn ŏl-ma-jyo?

How much is the entrance fee?

32 어린이/경로 할인이 있나요?
ŏ-rin-i / gyŏng-no hal-in i it-na-yo?

Do you have a discount for children/senior citizens?

33 외국인은 얼마죠?
oe-gug-in ŭn ŏl-ma-jyo?

How much is it for foreigners?

34 여기 들어가도 되나요?
yŏ-gi dŭl-ŏ-ga-do doe-na-yo?

Can I go in here?

35 바깥에서만 관람해주세요.
ba-ggat-e-sŏ man gwal-lam hae-ju-se-yo.

Please look only from the outside.

36 들어가면 안됩니다.
dŭl-ŏ-ga-myŏn an-doep-ni-da.

You can't go in.

37
조용히 해주세요.
jo-yong-hi hae-ju-se-yo.

Please keep quiet.

38
큰 소리로 말하면 안됩니다.
kŭn so-ri ro mal-ha-myŏn an-doep-ni-da.

(Lit) You can't talk in a loud voice.

= Please lower your voice.

39
만지면 안됩니다.
man-ji-myŏn an-doep-ni-da.

You can't touch (it).

40
기념품 가게는 어디에 있나요?
gi-nyŏm-pum ga-ge-nŭn ŏ-di-e it-na-yo?

(At) where is the souvenir shop?

41
기념품을 사고 싶습니다.
gi-nyŏm-pum ŭl sa-go ship-sŭp-ni-da.

I'd like to buy souvenirs.

42
입장권을 보여주세요.
ip-jang-ggwŏn ŭl bo-yŏ-ju-se-yo.

Please show me (your) admission ticket.

43
검색을 하겠습니다.
gŏm-saeg ŭl ha-get-ssŭp-ni-da.

I'm going to do a (security) scan.

44
음식은 반입이 안됩니다.
ŭm-shig ŭn ban-ib i an-doep-ni-da.

(Lit) Food is not allowed to be taken inside.

45
안에 식당이 있나요?
an-e shik-dang i it-na-yo?

Is there a restaurant inside?

46
문화적인 의미가 있습니다.
mun-hwa-jŏg-in ŭi-mi ga it-ssŭp-ni-da.

It has a cultural meaning/significance.

47
이런건 처음 봅니다.
i-rŏn gŏn chŏ-ŭm bop-ni-da.

(Lit) (It's my) first time seeing something like this.

= I've never seen anything like this.

48
경치 좋다!
gyŏng-chi jot-ta!

The view is good!

= What a view!

49
정말 멋집니다.
jŏng-mal mŏt-jip-ni-da..

It's really cool.

50
생각보다 멋집니다.
saeng-gak bo-da mŏt-jip-ni-da.

It's cooler than I thought.

51 정말 한국적이네요.
jŏng-mal han-guk-jŏg i-ne-yo.

It's really Korean (style).

52 아주 독특합니다.
a-ju dok-tŭk-hap-ni-da.

This is so unique.

53 이게 다예요?
i-ge da ye-yo?

Is this all?

54 별로네요.
byŏl-lo-ne-yo.

It's not that good.

55 실망스럽네요.
shil-mang-sŭ-rŏp-ne-yo.

It's disappointing.

56 괜히 왔어요.
gwen-hi wa-ssŏ-yo.

We came here for nothing.

정말 한국적이네요.
jŏng-mal han-guk-jŏg i-ne-yo.

Chapter 15. WEATHER

01 날씨가 어때요?
nal-shi ga ŏ-ttae-yo?

How's the weather?

02 날씨가 정말 좋네요!
nal-shi ga jŏng-mal jot-ne-yo!

(Lit) The weather is really nice!

=What beautiful weather!

03 매일 날씨가 이랬으면 좋겠어요.
mae-il nal-shi ga i-rae-sŭ-myŏn jo-ke-ssŏ-yo.

I wish the weather were like this every day.

04 날씨가 왜 이렇죠?
nal-shi ga wae i-rŏt-chyo?

(Lit) Why is the weather like this?

= What's wrong with the weather?

05 비가 오려나?
bi ga o-ryŏ-na?

(Lit) Will rain come?

= Is it going to rain?

06 하늘이 맑아요.
ha-nŭl i mal-ga-yo.

The sky is clear.

07 햇살이 따갑습니다.
hae-ssal i tta-gap-sŭp-ni-da.

(Lit) The sunlight stings.

= The sun is hot.

08 구름이 많이 꼈네요.
gu-rŭm i man-i ggyŏt-ne-yo.

(Lit) Lots of clouds hang over.

= It's overcast.

09 눈이 내린다!
nun i nae-rin-da!

(Lit) Snow's falling down! = It's snowing!

10 첫눈이다!
chŏt nun i-da!

It's the first snow!

11 비가 쏟아지네요!
bi ga sso-da-ji-ne-yo!

(Lit) Rain is pouring down!

= It's tipping down!

12 일기 예보가 틀렸어요.
il-gi ye-bo ga tŭl-lyŏ-sŏ-yo.

The weather forecast is wrong.

13 우산을 가져올걸!
u-san ŭl ga-jyŏ-ol-gŏl!

I should have brought an umbrella!

14 너무 덥네요/춥네요.
nŏ-mu dŏp-ne-yo/chup-ne-yo.

It's too hot/cold.

15 굉장히 습하네요/건조하네요.
goeng-jang-hi sŭp-ha-ne-yo / gŏn-jo-ha-ne-yo.

It's very humid/dry.

16 비가/눈이 그쳤나요?
bi ga / nun i gŭ-chyŏt-na-yo?

(Lit) Did the rain/snow stop?

= Did it stop raining/snowing?

17 이제 안오네요.
i-je an o-ne-yo.

(Lit) It's not coming now.

= It stopped raining/snowing.

18 내일은 날씨가 어떨까요?
nae-il ŭn nal-shi ga ŏ-ttŏl-gga-yo?

What will the weather be like tomorrow?

19 날씨가 정말 이상하네요.
nal-shi ga jŏng-mal i-sang-ha-ne-yo.

The weather is really weird.

20 서울 날씨는 어때요?
sŏ-ul nal-shi nŭn ŏ-ttae-yo?

How's the weather (in) Seoul?

21 비가/눈이 올 것 같아요.
bi ga / nun i ol gŏt gat-a-yo.

(Lit) It seems like rain/snow will come.

22 일기 예보 들으셨나요?
il-gi ye-bo dŭl-ŭ-shŏt-na-yo?

Have you heard the weather forecast?

23 일기 예보에 따르면 화창할 예정입니다.

il-gi ye-bo-e tta-rŭ-myŏn hwa-chang-hal ye-jŏng-ip-ni-da.

(Lit) According to the weather forecast, it's planned to be sunny.

24 태풍이 오고 있어요.

tae-pung i o-go i-ssŏ-yo.

The storm is coming.

25 소풍가기에 날씨가 어때요?

so-pung ga-gi-e nal-shi ga ŏ-ttae-yo?

How's the weather for going on a picnic?

26 오늘 몇 도예요?

o-nŭl myŏt do ye-yo?

(Lit) What is the degree today?

= What's the temperature today?

27 최고기온은/최저기온은 30도입니다.

choe-go gi-on ŭn/choe-jŏ gi-on ŭn sam-ship do ip-ni-da.

(Lit) The highest/lowest degree is 30 degrees.

28 날씨가 차차 좋아지고 있어요.

nal-shi ga cha-cha jo-a-ji-go i-ssŏ-yo.

The weather is gradually getting better.

29 아침내내 흐렸어요.

a-chim nae-nae hŭ-ryŏ-ssŏ-yo.

It's been cloudy during the whole morning.

30 날씨를 예측할 수 없네요.

nal-shi rŭl ye-chŭk hal su ŏp-ne-yo.

I can't predict the weather.

31 해가 점점 짧아지고/길어지고 있어요.

hae ga jŏm-jŏm jjal-ba-ji-go / gil-ŏ-ji-go i-ssŏ-yo.

The sun is gradually getting shorter/longer.

= The days are drawing in/out.

32 오후에 비가/눈이 올 거예요.

o-hu e bi ga / nun i ol gŏ-ye-yo.

(Lit) Rain/Snow will come in the afternoon.

33 날씨가 변덕스러워요.

nal-shi ga byŏn-dŏk-sŭ-rŏ-wŏ-yo.

The weather is fickle/changeable/uncertain.

34 날씨가 오락가락 하네요.

nal-shi ga o-rak-ga-rak ha-ne-yo.

(Lit) The weather is going back and forth.

= The weather keeps changing.

35 곧 좋아질 거예요.

got jo-a-jil gŏ-ye-yo.

It will get better soon.

36 하루종일 비가/눈이 오네요.
ha-ru-jong-il bi ga / nun i o-ne-yo.

(Lit) Rain/Snow is coming all day long.

= It's raining/snowing all day long.

37 기온이 많이 떨어졌어요.
gi-on i man-i ttŏl-ŏ-jyŏ-ssŏ-yo.

The temperature dropped a lot.

38 날씨가 따뜻하네요.
nal-shi ga tta-ttŭt-ha-ne-yo.

(Lit) The weather is warm.

= It's warm.

39 날씨가 맑겠습니다.
nal-shi ga mal-gget-sŭp-ni-da.

The weather will be clear.

40 일기 예보는 믿을 수 없습니다.
il-gi ye-bo nŭn mid-ŭl su-ga ŏp-sŭp-ni-da.

You can't trust the weather forecast.

41 한국 날씨 어때요?
han-guk nal-shi ŏ-ttae-yo?

How's the weather (in) Korea?

42 어떤 계절이 가장 좋아요?
ŏ-ttŏn gye-jŏl i ga-jang jo-a-yo?

Which season do you like the most?

43 봄이/여름이/가을이/겨울이 가장 좋아요.
bom i / yŏ-rŭm i / ga-ŭl i / gyŏ-ul i ga-jang jo-a-yo.

I like Spring/Summer/Fall/Winter the most.

44 곧 봄이 올 거예요.
got bom i ol gŏ-ye-yo.

Spring will come soon.

45 잎이 붉게 물드네요.
ip i bul-gge mul-dŭ-ne-yo.

The leaves are turning red.

46 황사가 옵니다.
hwang-sa ga op-ni-da.

The sandstorm is coming.

47 황사때문에 눈이 따가워요.
hwang-sa ttae-mun-e nun i tta-ga-wŏ-yo.

(My) eyes sting because of the sandstorm.

48 비가 오면 좋겠어요.
bi ga o-myŏn jo-ke-ssŏ-yo.

It'd be nice if the rain comes.

49 지금은 장마철이에요.
ji-gŭm ŭn jang-ma-chŏl i-e-yo.

It's a rainy season now.

50 이번 주부터 장마가 시작됩니다.
i-bŏn ju bu-tŏ jang-ma ga shi-jak-doep-ni-da.

The rainy season starts (from) this week.

51 쾌적한 날씨네요!
kwae-jŏk-han nal-shi ne-yo!

(Lit) It's pleasant weather!

= What pleasant/ideal weather it is!

52 날씨 정말 좋네요!
nal-shil jŏng-mal jot-ne-yo!

The weather is really good!

53 구름 하나 없어요.
gu-rŭm ha-na ŏp-sŏ-yo.

There isn't a single cloud!

54 땀이 나네요.
ttam i na-ne-yo.

(Lit) Sweat is coming out.

I'm sweating.

55 안개가 자욱하네요.
an-gae ga ja-uk-ha-ne-yo.

(Lit) It's filled with fog.

= It's really foggy.

56 바람이 많이 부네요.
ba-ram i man-i bu-ne-yo.

(Lit) The wind blows a lot.

= It's very windy.

57 공기가 안좋아요.
gong-gi ga an-jo-a-yo.

The air (quality) is not good.

58 눈이 많이 쌓였어요.
nun i man-i ssa-yŏ-ssŏ-yo.

Snow has accumulated a lot.

= Lots of snow have piled up.

59 길이 얼었어요.
gil i ŏl-ŏ-ssŏ-yo.

The road is frozen.

60 길이 미끄러워요.
gil i mi-ggŭ-rŏ-wŏ-yo.

The road is slippery.

Chapter 16. EMOTIONS

01 정말 기뻐요.
jŏng-mal gi-bbŏ-yo.

I'm really happy.

02 좋은 생각이에요!
jo-ŭn saeng-gag i-e-yo!

That's a great idea!

03 훌륭합니다.
hul-lyung-hap-ni-da.

It's fabulous.

04 화났어요?
hwa na-ssŏ-yo?

(Lit) Do you have anger?

= Are you upset?

05 많이 화났어요.
man-i hwa na-ssŏ-yo.

(Lit) I have a lot of anger.

= I'm very angry.

06 짜증나요.
jja-zŭng na-yo.

(Lit) I have irritation.

I'm really irritated.

07 열받았어요.
yŏl bad-a-ssŏ-yo.

(Lit) I've received heat.

= I'm pissed.

08 안심이 됩니다.
an-shim i doep-ni-da.

That's a relief.

09 놀랍군요!
nol-lap-gun-yo!

Incredible! / Amazing!

10 농담이죠?
nong-dam i-jyo?

(Lit) It's a joke, right?

= You are kidding me, right?

11 장난하지 마세요.
jang-nan ha-ji ma-se-yo.

(Lit) Please do not play with me.

= Quit playing.

12 믿을 수 없어!
mid-ŭl su ŏp-sŏ!

I can't believe it!

13 환상적이네요!
hwan-sang-jŏg i-ne-yo!

It's fantastic!

14 멋질 거예요!
mŏt-jil gŏ-ye-yo!

It will be cool!

15 진짜예요?
jin-jja ye-yo?

(Lit) Is it real?

= For real?

16 진심인가요?
jin-shim in-ga-yo?

(Lit) Is it (your) true intention?

= Are you serious?

17 흥미진진하네요.
hŭng-mi-jin-jin ha-ne-yo.

That's exciting!

18 끔찍해!
ggŭm-jjik-hae!

That's awful!

19 창피해!
chang-pi-hae!

What a shame!

20 이제 제발 그만해!
i-je je-bal gŭ-man-hae!

Please stop now!

21 매우 불쾌하네요.
mae-u bul-kwae-ha-ne-yo.

I'm extremely unhappy.

22 슬퍼요.
sŭl-pŏ-yo.

I'm sad.

23 정말 비참하네요.
jŏng-mal bi-cham-ha-ne-yo.

It's really miserable.

24 기분이 별로 좋지 않아요.
gi-bun i byŏl-lo jot-chi an-a-yo.

(Lit) (My) feelings are not especially good.

= I'm not in a good mood.

25 기분이 좋아요.
gi-bun i jo-a-yo.

(Lit) (My) feelings are good.

= I'm feeling good.

26 우울하네요.
u-ul-ha-ne-yo.

I feel down.

27 실망이에요.
shil-mang i-e-yo.

(Lit) It's a disappointment.

= I'm disappointed.

28 당신에게 실망했어요.
dang-shin e-ge shil-mang-hae-ssŏ-yo.

I'm disappointed in you.

29 애석하네요.
ae-sŏk-ha-ne-yo.

That's a pity.

30 저런, 안됐네요.
jŏ-rŏn, an-doet-ne-yo.

Oh my, that's too bad.

31 운이 나빴어요.
un i na-bba-ssŏ-yo.

(Lit) The luck was bad. = That was unlucky.

32 그 말을 들으니 유감입니다.
gŭ mal ŭl dŭl-ŭ-ni yu-gam-ip-ni-da.

(Lit) I'm sorry to hear that saying.

= I'm sorry to hear that.

33 저는 당신 편이에요.
jŏ nŭn dang-shin pyŏn i-e-yo.

I am (on) your side.

34 실망하지 마세요.
shil-mang ha-ji ma-se-yo.

Don't be disappointed.

35 무슨 일이지요?
mu-sŭn il i-ji-yo?

What is the matter?

36 뭐가 잘못되었나요?
mwŏ ga jal-mot doe-ŏt-na-yo?

Is there anything wrong?

37 괜찮아요?
goen-chan-a-yo?
Are you okay? / Is it okay?

38 걱정하지 마세요.
gŏk-jŏng ha-ji ma-se-yo.
Don't worry.

39 무엇 때문에 걱정이세요?
mu-ŏt ttae-mun-e gŏk-jŏng-i-se-yo?
(Lit) Because of what are you concerned?
= What's bothering you?

40 무슨 문제 있나요?
mu-sŭn mun-je it-na-yo?
Is there any problem?

41 빨리 해결하시기를 바래요.
bbal-li hae-gyŏl-ha-shi-gi rŭl ba-rae-yo.
(Lit) I hope for you to resolve (it) soon.

42 대단히 감사합니다.
dae-dan-hi gam-sa-hap-ni-da.
Thank you very much.

43 모든 것에 감사드려요.
mo-dŭn gŏ se gam-sa-dŭ-ryŏ-yo.
Thank you for everything.

44 도와주셔서 감사합니다.
do-wa-ju-shŏ-sŏ gam-sa-hap-ni-da.
Thank you for helping me.

45 저에게 큰 도움이 되어주셨어요.
jŏ e-ge kŭn do-um i doe-ŏ-ju-shŏ-ssŏ-yo.
You've been a great help to me.

46 초대해 주셔서 감사합니다.
cho-dae-hae ju-shŏ-sŏ gam-sa-hap-ni-da.
Thank you for inviting me.

47 고맙습니다.
go-map-sŭp-ni-da.
Thank you.

48 정말 친절하시네요.
jŏng-mal chin-jŏl-ha-shi-ne-yo.
(Lit) You are really kind.
= That's very kind of you.

49 저야말로 감사합니다.
jŏ-ya-mal-lo gam-sa-hap-ni-da.
(Lit) It is ME who's thankful.
= Thank YOU.

50 천만에요.
chŏn-man-e-yo.
You're welcome.

51 미안합니다.
mi-an-hap-ni-da.
I'm sorry.

52 죄송합니다.
joe-song-hap-ni-da.
I apologize.

53 정말 죄송합니다.
jŏng-mal joe-song-hap-ni-da.
I sincerely apologize.

54 정말 미안합니다.
jŏng-mal mi-an-hap-ni-da.
I'm really sorry.

55 늦어서 죄송합니다.
nŭ-zŏ-sŏ joe-song-hap-ni-da.
I'm sorry for being late.

56 기다리게 해서 죄송해요.
gi-da-ri-ge hae-sŏ joe-song-hae-yo.
I'm sorry to have kept you waiting.

57 제 실수예요.
je shil-su ye-yo.
It's my mistake.

58 제 실수를 사과드립니다.
je shil-su rŭl sa-gwa-dŭ-rip-ni-da.
I apologize (for) my mistake.

59 너무 시끄럽게 해서 죄송합니다.
nŏ-mu shi-ggŭ-rŏp-ge hae-sŏ joe-song-hap-ni-da.
I apologize for being too loud/noisy.

60 그런 의도가 아니었어요.
gŭ-run ŭi-do ga a-ni-ŏ-ssŏ-yo.
(Lit) It was not such intention.
= That was not my intention.

61 당연하죠!
dang-yŏn-ha-jyo!
Of course!

62 물론이죠!
mul-lon-i-jyo!
Absolutely!

63 미쳤어요?
mi-chyŏ-ssŏ-yo?
Are you crazy?

64 정신 나갔어요?
jŏng-shin na-ga-ssŏ-yo?
(Lit) Did (your) mind go out?
= Are you out of your mind?

65   화내지 마세요.
hwa-nae-ji ma-se-yo.

Don't get upset.

66   무서워요.
mu-sŏ-wŏ-yo.

It's scary / You're scary.

67   너무 웃겨요.
nŏ-mu ut-gyŏ-yo.

It's too funny.

68   정말 재밌어요.
jŏng-mal jae-mi-ssŏ-yo.

It's really fun.

69   마음이 아파요.
ma-ŭm i   a-pa-yo.

(Lit) (My) mind aches/hurts. = I'm heartbroken.

Chapter 17. AT WORK

01 신입사원 김철수입니다.
shin-ip-sa-wŏn kim chŏl-su ip-ni-da.

I'm Kim Cheol-su, a new employee/recruit.

02 많이 가르쳐주세요.
man-i ga-rŭ-chyŏ-ju-se-yo.

(Lit) Please teach me a lot.

= I hope to learn a lot from you.

03 인턴으로 들어왔습니다.
in-tŏn ŭ-ro dŭl-ŏ-wa-sŭp-ni-da.

(Lit) I've entered as an intern.

= I'm joining as an intern.

04 마케팅부서에서 일하게 되었습니다.
ma-ke-ting bu-sŏ e-sŏ il-ha-ge doe-ŏ-ssŭp-ni-da.

I've been made (= assigned) to work in the marketing department.

05 함께 일하게 되어 영광입니다.
ham-gge il-ha-ge doe-ŏ yŏng-gwang ip-ni-da.

(Lit) It's an honor (for being able) to work together.

= I'm honored to work with you.

06 이 전에는 삼성에서 일했어요.
i jŏn-e-nŭn sam-sŏng e-sŏ il-hae-ssŏ-yo.

(Lit) I worked at Samsung before this.

= I used to work at OO before coming here.

07 출근/퇴근은 몇시인가요?
chul-gŭn/toe-gŭn ŭn myŏ-sshi in-ga-yo?

What time is clock- in/out?

08 점심 시간은 몇시부터인가요?
jŏm-shim shi-gan ŭn myŏ-sshi bu-tŏ in-ga-yo?

(Lit) What time is lunchtime from?

09 제 자리는 어디죠?
je ja-ri nŭn ŏ-di-jyo?

(Lit) Where is my seat?

= Where is my cubicle/desk?

10 사원증을 만들어드릴게요.
sa-wŏn-tzŭng ŭl man-dŭl-ŏ dŭ-ril-gge-yo.

I will make you an employee card.

11 계약서에 서명해주세요.
gye-yak-sŏ e sŏ-myŏng hae-ju-se-yo.

Please sign the contract.

12 연봉은 얼마죠?.
yŏn-bong ŭn ŏl-ma-jyo?

How much is the (annual) salary?

13 월급은 통장으로 보내드립니다.
wŏl-gŭb ŭn tong-jang ŭ-ro bo-nae-dŭ-rip-ni-da.

(Lit) We send (monthly) payment to (your) account.

14 휴가는 일년에 며칠인가요?
hyu-ga nŭn il-nyŏn e myŏ-chil in-ga-yo?

(Lit) How many vacation days is it a year?

= How many vacation days do I get a year?

15 구내식당은 어디죠?
gu-nae-shik-dang ŭn ŏ-di-jyo?

Where is the cafeteria?

16 야근을 많이 하나요?
ya-gŭn ŭl man-i ha-na-yo?

(Lit) Do we do a lot of overtime at night?

17 프로젝트가 많아요.
pŭ-ro-jek-tŭ ga man-a-yo.

We have/There are a lot of projects.

18 우리 팀장님은 깐깐해요.
u-ri tim-jang-nim ŭn ggan-ggan-hae-yo.

Our manager is picky/fastidious.

19 우리 사장님은 개방적이에요.
u-ri sa-jang-nim ŭn gae-bang-jŏg i-e-yo.

Our boss is open-minded.

20 사내 연애는 금지예요.
sa-nae yŏn-ae nŭn gŭm-ji-ye-yo.

(Lit) Inside-office romances are prohibited.

= Dating at work is prohibited.

21 담배를 피려면 옥상으로 가세요.
dam-bae rŭl pi-ryŏ-myŏn ok-sang-ŭ-ro ga-se-yo.

(Lit) If you are going to smoke a cigarette, go to the rooftop.

22 복장은 정장/캐쥬얼 입니다.
bok-jang ŭn jŏng-jang/kae-yju-ŏl ip-ni-da.

The dress code is suit/casual.

23 탕비실은 어디인가요?
tang-bi-shil ŭn ŏ-di-in-ga-yo?

Where is the office pantry?

24 업무 보고를 해주세요.
ŏp-mu bo-go rŭl hae-ju-se-yo.

Please give me the business/activity report.

25 프레젠테이션 준비를 합시다.
pŭ-re-jen-te-i-shŏn jun-bi rŭl hap-shi-da.

Let's get ready (for) the presentation.

26 아주 중요한 미팅이에요.
a-ju jung-yo-han mi-ting i-e-yo.

It's a very important meeting.

27 여기선 원래 그렇게 해요.
yŏ-gi-sŏn wŏl-lae gŭ-rŏt-ke hae-yo.

(Lit) (We) usually do like that at here.

= That's how we do it around here.

28 이렇게 하면 되나요?
i-rŏt-ke ha-myŏn doe-na-yo?

(Lit) Is it okay if I do like this?

29 업무가 많네요/적네요.
ŏp-mu ga man-ne-yo/jŏk-ne-yo.

There is a lot of/little work.

30 퇴근 해도 될까요?
toe-gŭn hae-do doel-gga-yo?

May I get off work?

= Do you mind if I leave?

31 제가 더 도와드릴 일이 있을까요?
je ga dŏ do-wa-dŭ-ril il i i-ssŭl-gga-yo?

(Lit) Would there be a work I can help you more with?

32 좋은 동료가 있어서 기쁘네요.
jo-ŭn dong-nyo ga i-ssŏ-sŏ gi-bbŭ-ne-yo.

(Lit) I'm happy because I have a good colleague.

33 내일은 휴일이라 출근 안해도 되요.
nae-il ŭn hyu-il i-ra chul-gŭn an-hae-do doe-yo.

You don't have to come to work because tomorrow is a holiday.

34 오늘 결근이에요.
o-nŭl gyŏl-gŭn i-e-yo.

(I am/He is/She is) absent today.

35 몸이 아파서 조퇴하려고요.
mom i a-pa-sŏ jo-toe ha-ryŏ-go-yo.

(Lit) I'm planning to leave early because (my) body aches.

= I'm going to leave early because I'm not feeling well.

36 제 업무 좀 대신 해주세요.
je ŏp-mu jom dae-shin hae-ju-se-yo.

(Lit) Please do my work on my behalf.

= Can you fill in for me?

37 왜 퇴근 안하세요?
oe toe-gŭn an-ha-se-yo?

Why aren't you getting off work?

38 오늘 야근 하시나요?
o-nŭl ya-gŭn ha-shi-na-yo?

Are you working overtime at night today?

39 경비처리 하면 되요.
gyŏng-bi chŏ-ri ha-myŏn doe-yo.

It can be written off as a business expense.

40 빨리 해주세요.
bbal-li hae-ju-se-yo.

Please do it quickly.

41 오늘까지 처리 해야해요.
o-nŭl gga-ji chŏ-ri hae-ya-hae-yo.

It has to be taken care of by today.

42 저에게 이메일로 보내주세요.
jŏ e-ge i-mae-il lo bo-nae-ju-se-yo.

Send it to me via email, please.

43 회의실로 오세요.
hoe-ŭi-shil lo o-se-yo.

Come to the meeting room, please.

44 그렇게 하면 안돼요.
gŭ-rŏt-ke ha-myŏn an-doe-yo.

(Lit) It's not okay if you do it like that.

= You shouldn't do it like that.

45 결재해주세요.
gyŏl-jae hae-ju-se-yo.

Please approve/authorize.

46 사장님께 보고하세요.
sa-jang-nim-gge bo-go ha-se-yo.

Please report to the boss.

47 이 서류를 복사해주세요.
i sŏ-ryu rŭl bok-sa hae-ju-se-yo.

Please make copies of this document.

48 좀 쉬었다 합시다.
jom shwi-ŏt-da hap-shi-da.

(Lit) Let's do it after resting a little.

= Let's take a quick break.

49 집에서 마무리 할게요.
jib e-sŏ ma-mu-ri hal-gge-yo.

I'll finish it at home.

50 재택근무 하려고요.
jae-taek-gŭn-mu ha-ryŏ-go-yo.

I'll work from home.

51 내일도 사무실에 나와주세요.
nae-il do sa-mu-shil e na-wa-ju-se-yo.

(Lit) Come out to the office (= work) tomorrow, please.

52 오늘 회식 있습니다.
o-nŭl hoe-shik it-ssŭp-ni-da.

There is a company get-together today.

53 회식에 꼭 가야하나요?
hoe-shig e ggok ga-ya ha-na-yo?

Do I have to go to the company get-together?

54 물론이죠. 빠지면 안돼요.
mul-lon-i-jyo. bba-ji-myŏn an-doe-yo.

(Lit) Of course. It's not okay if you miss it.

55 오늘 아파서 출근 못할 것 같아요.
o-nŭl a-pa-sŏ chul-gŭn mot-hal gŏt gat-a-yo.

(Lit) I think I can't go to work because I'm feeling sick today.

56 결근계를 작성해주세요.
gyŏl-gŭn-gye rŭl jak-sŏng hae-ju-se-yo.

Please fill out a report of absence.

57 너무 열심히 일하지 마세요.
nŏ-mu yŏl-shim-hi il ha-ji ma-se-yo.

Don't work too hard.

58 깜빡 졸았어요.
ggam-bbak jol-at-ŏ-yo.

I dozed off for a brief moment.

= I fell asleep.

59 먼저 퇴근할게요.
mŏn-jŏ toe-gŭn hal-gge-yo.

(Lit) I'll get off work first (= before you).

= I'm leaving.

60 수고하세요!
su-go ha-se-yo!

(Lit) Continue taking the trouble!

= Take it easy. / See you.

61 팀장님보다 먼저 퇴근하면 안돼요.
tim-jang-nim bo-da mŏn-jŏ toe-gŭn ha-myŏn an-doe-yo.

(Lit) It's not okay if you leave work earlier than the boss.

62 다들 그렇게 해요.
da-dŭl gŭ-rŏt-ke hae-yo.

(Lit) Everyone does it like that.

= That's how it's done around here.

63 신입사원 교육을 하겠습니다.
shin-ip-sa-wŏn gyo-yug ŭl ha-get-ssŭp-ni-da.

We will have a new employee training.

64 승진 축하드립니다!
sŭng-jin chuk-ha-dŭ-rip-ni-da!

Congratulations (on your) promotion!

65 인사평가에 반영 될거예요.
in-sa-pyŏng-gga e ban-yŏng doel-ggŏ-ye-yo.

It will be reflected in the employee evaluation.

66 인사과에 가서 말해보세요.
in-sa-ggwa e ga-sŏ mal-hae-bo-se-yo.

(Lit) Go try talking to the HR department.

67 어느 분께 여쭤보면 될까요?
ŏ-nŭ bun gge yŏ-jjwŏ-bo-myŏn doel-gga-yo?

(Lit) To which person should I ask?

68 월급이 아직 안 들어왔어요.
wŏl-gŭb i a-jik an dŭl-ŏ-wa-ssŏ-yo.

(Lit) The paycheck hasn't come in yet.

= I still haven't received my paycheck yet.

69 월급이 올랐어요.
wŏl-gŭb i ol-la-ssŏ-yo.

(Lit) (My) monthly pay went up.

= I received a raise.

70 저는 퇴사하려고요.
jŏ nŭn toe-sa ha-ryŏ-go-yo.

(Lit) I am planning to leave the company.

= I'm going to resign/quick the job.

71 다른 곳으로 이직하려고요.
da-rŭn go sŭ-ro i-jik ha-ryŏ-go-yo.

(I am) planning to move over to a different place (= company).

72 더 좋은 조건을 주는 곳을 찾았어요.
dŏ jo-ŭn jo-ggŏn ŭl ju-nŭn go sŭl cha-ja-ssŏ-yo.

I found a place that gives me a better offer.

73 이직 제의가 들어왔어요.
i-jik je-ŭi ga dŭl-ŏ-wa-ssŏ-yo.

(Lit) An offer to move to a different company came in.

= I've got a job offer from a different company.

74 그 분은 예전에 그만 두셨어요.
gŭ bun ŭn ye-jŏn-e gŭ-man du-shŏ-ssŏ-yo.

That person (= he/she) quit a while ago.

118

Chapter 18. POLICE STATION

01 도와주세요!
do-wa-ju-se-yo!

Please help (me)!

02 도움이 필요합니다.
do-um i pil-yo-hap-ni-da.

(I) need help.

03 지갑을 도둑맞았어요.
ji-gab ŭl do-dug-ma-za-ssŏ-yo.

(I) had (my) wallet/purse lifted/stolen.

04 여권을 잃어버렸어요.
yŏ-ggwŏn ŭl il-ŏ-bŏ-ryŏ-ssŏ-yo.

I lost/misplaced (my) passport.

05 소매치기를 당했어요.
so-mae-chi-gi rŭl dang-hae-ssŏ-yo.

I got (my) pocket-picked.

06 지하철에 지갑을 놓고 내렸어요.
ji-ha-chŏl e ji-gab ŭl not-ko nae-ryŏ-ssŏ-yo.

(I) got off with (my) wallet left on the subway.

07 강도를 당했어요.
gang-do rŭl dang-hae-ssŏ-yo.

I got robbed.

08 이 사람이 저를 폭행했습니다.
i sa-ram i jŏ rŭl pok-haeng-haet-ssŭp-ni-da.

This man assaulted me.

09 폭행 당했어요.
pok-haeng dang-hae-ssŏ-yo.

I got assaulted.

10 바로 저 사람/이 사람이에요!
ba-ro jŏ sa-ram / i sa-ram i-e-yo!

That/This is the man right there!
/ This is him/her right here!

11 어떻게 생겼나요?
ŏ-ttŏ-ke saeng-gyŏt-na-yo?

How/What does (he/she) look like?

12 인상착의를 알려주세요.
in-sang-chag-ŭi rŭl al-lyŏ-ju-se-yo.

Please tell me (his/her) features and clothes.

13 잘 기억이 안나요.
jal gi-ŏg i an-na-yo.

I don't remember well.

14 대충 이렇게 생겼어요.
dae-chung i-rŏt-ke saeng-gyŏ-ssŏ-yo.

(He/She) looks roughly like this.

15 특징을 말씀해주세요.
tŭk-jing ŭl mal-ssŭm-hae-ju-se-yo.

Please tell me (his/her) features.

16 찾을 수 있을까요?
cha-zŭl su i-ssŭl-gga-yo?

Can you find (him/her)?

17 쉽지 않겠네요.
ship-ji an-ket-ne-yo.

It's not going to be easy.

18 여기 조서를 작성해주세요.
yŏ-gi jo-sŏ rŭl jak-sŏng-hae-ju-se-yo.

Please fill out the report here.

19 돈은 얼마나 들어있었죠?
don ŭn ŏl-ma-na dŭl-ŏ-i-ssŏt-jyo?

(Lit) How much money was contained (= in there?)?

20 가방에는 무엇이 들어있었죠?
ga-bang e nŭn mu-ŏ shi dŭl-ŏ-i-ssŏt-jyo?

(Lit) What was contained in the bag?

21 한국에 지인이 있나요?
han-gug e ji-in i it-na-yo?

Do you have anyone you know in Korea?

22 비상 연락처가 있나요?
bi-sang yŏl-lak-chŏ ga it-na-yo?

Do you have emergency contact?

23 어디에서 그랬나요?
ŏ-di e-sŏ gŭ-raet-na-yo?

(Lit) (From) where did it happen?

= Where did it take place?

24 언제 그랬나요?
ŏn-je gŭ-raet-na-yo?

When did it happen?

= When did it take place?

25 정확한 위치를 알려주세요.
jŏng-hwak-han wi-chi rŭl al-lyŏ-ju-se-yo.

Please give me the precise location.

26 경찰서로 갑시다.
gyŏng-chal-sŏ ro gap-shi-da.

Let's go to the police station.

27 저를 협박했어요.
jŏ rŭl hyŏp-bak-hae-ssŏ-yo.

(He/She) threatened me.

28 지금 협박하는건가요?
ji-gŭm hyŏp-bak-ha-nŭn-gŏn-ga-yo?

Are you threatening (me) now?

29 경찰에 신고할겁니다.
gyŏng-chal e shin-go hal-gŏp-ni-da.

I'm going to report (you) to the police.

30 경찰을 불러주세요.
gyŏng-chal ŭl bul-lŏ-ju-se-yo.

Please call the police.

31 위험에 처해있습니다.
wi-hŏm e chŏ-hae-it-ssŭp-ni-da.

(Lit) (I am/We are) put in danger.

32 빨리 출동해주세요.
bbal-li chul-dong-hae-ju-se-yo.

(Lit) Please get dispatched (to here) quickly.

= Please get here quickly.

33 동영상을 촬영했습니다.
dong-yŏng-sang ŭl chwal-yŏng-haet-ssŭp-ni-da.

I recorded a video clip.

34 전부 녹음했습니다.
jŏn-bu nog-ŭm-haet-ssŭp-ni-da.

(I) (voice) recorded everything.

35 이게 증거입니다.
i-ge jŭng-gŏ ip-ni-da.

This is the evidence.

36 이 사람은 거짓말을 하고 있어요.
i sa-ram ŭn gŏ-jit-mal ŭl ha-go-i-ssŏ-yo.

This man/person is lying.

121

37 전혀 거짓말이 아닙니다.
jŏn-hyŏ gŏ-jit-mal i a-nip-ni-da.
It's not a lie at all.

38 빨리 범인을 잡아주세요.
bbal-li bŏm-in ŭl jab-a-ju-se-yo.
Please catch the suspect quickly.

39 처벌을 원합니다.
chŏ-bŏl ŭl wŏn-hap-ni-da.
I want to press charges.

40 처벌을 원치 않습니다.
chŏ-bŏl ŭl wŏn-chi an-ssŭp-ni-da.
I don't want to press charges.

41 꼭 잡아주세요!
ggok jab-a-ju-se-yo!
Please catch (him/her) at any cost!

42 저를 폭행하려 했습니다.
jŏ rŭl pok-haeng ha-ryŏ haet-ssŭp-ni-da.
(He/She) tried to assault me.

43 저의 지갑을 훔치려 했습니다.
jŏ-ŭi ji-gab ŭl hum-chi ryŏ haet-ssŭp-ni-da.
(He/She) tried to steal my wallet.

44 현장에서 잡았어요.
hyŏn-jang e-sŏ jab-a-ssŏ-yo.
(Lit) I caught (him/her) on the spot.
= I caught him/her red-handed.

45 다 봤어요.
da bwa-ssŏ-yo.
(I) saw it all.

46 이 사람이/저 사람이 범인입니다.
i sa-ram i / jŏ sa-ram i bŏm-in ip-ni-da.
This man/That man is the criminal.

47 도망갔습니다.
do-mang-gat-ssŭp-ni-da.
(He/She) ran away.

48 놓쳤어요.
not-chyŏt-ssŏ-yo.
We lost him.

49 담당 형사를 배정하겠습니다.
dam-dang hyŏng-sa rŭl bae-jŏng ha-get-ssŭp-ni-da.
We will assign a detective (who's in charge).

50 조사가 필요하면 연락드리겠습니다.
jo-sa ga pil-yo-ha-myŏn yŏl-lak-dŭ-ri-get-ssŭp-ni-da.
We will contact you if we need an investigation.

Chapter 19. FRIENDSHIP

01 힘내!
him nae!

(Lit) Up (your) power!

= Cheer up!

02 그런거 때문에 기죽지 마.
gŭ-rŏn gŏ ttae-mun-e gi-juk-ji ma.

Don't feel small because of things like that.

03 고개 들어.
go-gae dŭl-ŏ.

(Lit) Lift (your) chin.

= Keep your chin up.

04 기운내.
gi-un nae.

(Lit) Up (your) energy.

= Cheer up!

05 누구나 실수 할 수 있어.
nu-gu-na shil-su hal su i-ssŏ.

Anyone can make a mistake.

06 나였어도 그렇게 했을거야.
na-yŏ-ssŏ do gŭ-rŏt-ke hae-ssŭl-gŏ-ya.

(Lit) I would have done so too if I were you.

07 너는 잘못한거 없어.
nŏ nŭn jal-mot-han gŏ ŏp-ssŏ.

(Lit) There isn't anything you did wrong.

08 그냥 운이 없었다고 생각해.
gŭ-nyang un i ŏp-ssŏt-da-go saeng-gak-hae.

(Lit) Just think that you didn't have luck.

= It was just not your day.

09 너는 최선을 다했어.
nŏ nŭn choe-sŏn ŭl da-hae-ssŏ.

You did (your) best.

10 다음에는 더 잘 될거야.
da-ŭm-e nŭn dŏ jal doel-gŏ-ya.

(Lit) It will be done better next time.

11 아무도 신경 안써.
a-mu-do shin-gyŏng an-ssŏ.

(Lit) Anyone doesn't care.

= No one cares.

12 걱정하지마.
gŏk-jŏng ha-ji-ma.

Don't worry.

13 긍정적으로 생각해.
gŭng-jŏng-jŏg-ŭ-ro saeng-gak-hae.

Think positively.

14 좋은 기운을 보낸다.
jo-ŭn gi-un ŭl bo-naen-da.

Sending (you) good vibes.

15 너에겐 내가 있잖아.
nŏ-e-gen nae ga it-ja-na.

I am (here) for you.

= You've got a friend in me.

16 너를 사랑하는 사람들을 생각해.
nŏ rŭl sa-rang-ha-nŭn sa-ram-dŭl ŭl saeng-gak-hae.

Think (of the) people who love you.

17 이건 정말 아무것도 아니야.
i-gŏn jŏng-mal a-mu-gŏt-do a-ni-ya.

This isn't really anything.

18 큰 그림을 봐야지.
kŭn gŭ-rim ŭl bwa-ya-ji.

You have to see the big picture.

19 아직 기회는 남아있어.
a-jik gi-hoe nŭn nam-a-i-ssŏ.

There is still a chance left.

20 너의 능력을 과소평가 하지마.
nŏ-ŭi nŭng-nyŏg ŭl gwa-so-pyŏng-ga ha-ji-ma.

Don't underestimate your abilities.

21 너는 네가 생각하는 것보다 대단해.
nŏ nŭn ne ga saeng-gak-ha-nŭn gŏt bo-da dae-dan-hae.
*while 네 is supposed to be pronounced as "ne", in real
life most Korean speakers pronounce it as "ni".

You are greater than what you think.

22 너는 정말 멋진 녀석이야.
nŏ nŭn jŏng-mal mŏt-jin nyŏ-sŏg i-ya.

You are really a cool dude.

124

23 네가 힘들땐 내가 도와줄게.
ne ga him-dŭl ttaen nae ga do-wa-jul-ge.

I'll help you when you are in need.

24 도움이 필요하면 언제든지 말해.
do-um i pil-yo ha-myŏn ŏn-je-dŭn-ji mal-hae.

Tell me whenever you need help

25 술 한잔 하러 가자!
sul han-jan ha-rŏ ga-ja!

(Lit) Let's go have a glass of drink!

= Let's go grab a drink!

26 그 사람도 후회하고 있을거야.
gŭ sa-ram-do hu-hoe-ha-go i-ssŭl-gŏ-ya.

That person must be regretting (it) too.

27 전혀 걱정하지 않아도 돼.
jŏn-hyŏ gŏk-jŏng ha-ji an-a-do doe.

You don't have to worry at all.

28 다음에 더 잘하면 되지!
da-ŭm-e dŏ jal-ha-myŏn doe-ji!

(Lit) It's fine if you do better next time!

= You can do better next time!

29 내일은 내일의 태양이 뜰거야.
nae-il ŭn nae-il ŭi tae-yang i ttŭl-gŏ-ya.

(Lit) Tomorrow's sun will rise tomorrow.

= After all, Tomorrow is another day!

30 고민 하지마.
go-min ha-ji ma.

Don't be concerned.

31 우리 모두 너를 믿어!
u-ri mo-du nŏ rŭl mid-ŏ!

We all believe you!

32 나는 언제나 너를 믿어!
na nŭn ŏn-je-na nŏ rŭl mid-ŏ!

I always believe (in) you!

33 옳은 일을 하리라고 믿는다.
ol-ŭn il ŭl ha-ri-ra-go mit-nŭn-da.

I believe/trust that you will do the right thing.

34 유혹에 빠지지 말아라.
yu-hog e bba-ji-ji mal-a-ra.

Don't fall into temptation.

35 친구로써 말하는데,
chin-gu ro-ssŏ mal-ha-nŭn-de.

I'm telling you as a friend,

36 내 조언을 잊지마.
nae jo-ŏn ŭl it-ji-ma.

Don't forget my advice.

37 너를 위해서 하는 말이야.
nŏ rŭl wi-hae-sŏ ha-nŭn mal i-ya.

(Lit) It's a statement with your interest at heart.

38 서운하게 생각하지마.
sŏ-un-ha-ge saeng-gak ha-ji-ma.

Don't think (= feel) bummed out.

39 좋은 약은 입에 쓴거야.
jo-ŭn yag ŭn i be ssŭn-gŏ-ya.

(Lit) Good medicine is bitter to the mouth.

= Helpful advice can be displeasing to the ear.

40 같이 노력하자.
ga-chi no-ryŏk ha-ja.

Let's try hard together.

Chapter 20. DATING/ROMANCE

01 내일 시간 어때요?
nae-il shi-gan ŏ-ttae-yo?

(Lit) How's (your) time tomorrow?

= What are your plans for tomorrow?

02 내일 뭐해요?
nae-il mwŏ-hae-yo?

What are you doing tomorrow?

03 주말 계획 있어요?
ju-mal gye-hoek i-ssŏ-yo?

Do you have plans (for) the weekend?

04 별거 없어요.
byŏl gŏ ŏp-ssŏ-yo.

There isn't anything special.

05 그러면 우리 데이트 할까요?
gŭ-rŏ-myŏn u-ri de-i-tŭ hal-gga-yo?

Shall we go on a date, then?

06 저녁 같이 먹을까요?
jŏ-nyŏk ga-chi mŏg-ŭl-gga-yo?

Shall we eat (= have) dinner together?

07 제가 맛있는 곳을 알고 있어요.
je ga ma-shit-nŭn go sŭl al-go-i-ssŏ-yo.

(Lit) I know a delicious place.

08 맛집을 알아요.
mat-jib ŭl al-a-yo.

I know a hole-in-the-wall place.

127

09 정말 마음에 드실거예요.
jŏng-mal ma-ŭm e dŭ-shil-gŏ-ye-yo.

(Lit) It will really fit to (your) heart.

= You will really love it.

10 남자친구/여자친구 있어요?
nam-ja-chin-gu / yŏ-ja-chin-gu i-ssŏ-yo?

Do you have a boyfriend/girlfriend?

11 만나는 사람 있어요?
man-na-nŭn sa-ram i-ssŏ-yo?

(Lit) Do you have anyone (you are) meeting?

= Are you seeing anyone?

12 아니요, 싱글이에요.
a-ni-yo, sing-gŭl i-e-yo.

No, I'm single.

13 네, 남자친구/여자친구 있어요.
ne, nam-ja-chin-gu / yŏ-ja-chin-gu i-ssŏ-yo.

Yes, I have a boyfriend/girlfriend.

14 저는 이미 결혼했어요.
jŏ nŭn i-mi gyŏl-hon-hae-ssŏ-yo.

I am already married.

15 죄송하지만 제 타입이 아니에요.
joe-song-ha-ji-man je ta-ib i a-ni-e-yo.

I'm sorry but (you're) not my type.

16 완전히 제 타입이에요.
wan-jŏn-hi je ta-ib i-e-yo.

You are completely my type.

17 첫눈에 반했어요.
chŏt-nun e ban-hae-ssŏ-yo.

I fell in love at first sight.

/ It was love at first sight.

18 한번 만나보고 싶어요.
han-bŏn man-na-bo-go ship-ŏ-yo.

(Lit) I'd like to give a shot at meeting you.

= I'd like to get to know more about you.

19 우리 사귈까요?
u-ri sa-gwil-gga-yo?

(Lit) Shall we go out?

= Will you go out with me?

20 제 남자친구/여자친구 할래요?
je nam-ja-chin-gu / yŏ-ja-chin-gu hal-lae-yo?

(Lit) Do you want to be my boyfriend/girlfriend?

21 연락처 알려주실 수 있어요?
yŏl-lak-chŏ al-lyŏ-ju-shil su i-ssŏ-yo?

(Lit) Could you tell me (your) contact info?

22 세상에서 가장 예뻐요.
se-sang e-sŏ ga-jang ye-bbŏ-yo.

You are the prettiest in the world.

23 정말 잘생겼어요.
jŏng-mal jal-saeng-gyŏ-ssŏ-yo.

You are really handsome.

24 제 이상형이에요.
je i-sang-hyŏng i-e-yo.

(Lit) (You) are my ideal type.

= You are my Mr. Right/Ms. Right.

25 둘이 정말 잘 어울려요.
dul i jŏng-mal jal ŏ-ul-lyŏ-yo.

You two really look good together.

26 이제부터 우리 커플이에요.
i-je bu-tŏ u-ri kŏ-pŭl i-e-yo.

From now on, we are a couple.

27 손 잡아도 될까요?
son jab-a-do doel-gga-yo?

May I hold (your) hand?

28 더치페이 해요.
dŏ-chi-pe-i hae-yo.

Let's go dutch.

29 아니에요, 제가 살게요.
a-ni-e-yo, je ga sal-gge-yo.

(Lit) No, I will buy.

= No, I will pick up the tab.

30 이건 제 마음이에요.
i-gŏn je ma-ŭm i-e-yo.

(Lit) This is my heart.

= This is from my heart.

31 선물이 마음에 들지 모르겠네요.
sŏn-mul i ma-ŭm e dŭl-ji mo-rŭ-get-ne-yo.

(Lit) I don't know if the gift will fit to (your) heart.

= I don't know if you will the gift.

32 아니 뭘 이런걸 다!
a-ni mwŏl i-rŏn-gŏl da!

Oh no, what are all these!

33 정말 이러지 않으셔도 괜찮은데.
jŏng-mal i-rŏ-ji an-ŭ-shŏ-do gwen-chan-ŭn-de.

(Lit) It's fine if you really don't do this.

= You shouldn't have done this.

34 마음이 중요하죠.
ma-ŭm i jung-yo-ha-jyo.

It's the thought that's important (= counts).

35 마음만으로 충분해요.
ma-ŭm man-ŭ-ro chung-bun-hae-yo.

(Lit) Just (your) thoughts are enough.

= I appreciate the thought.

129

36 감사히 받을게요.
gam-sa-hi bad-ŭl-gge-yo.

I will gratefully accept it.

= It's gratefully received.

37 오늘이 우리 기념일이에요.
o-nŭl i u-ri gi-nyŏm il-i-e-yo.

Today is our anniversary.

38 무슨 기념일이요?
mu-sŭn gi-nyŏm-il i-yo?

What anniversary is it?

39 만난지 100일 되었어요.
man-nan-ji baeg il doe-ŏ-ssŏ-yo.

It's been 100 days since we met.

40 우리의 만남을 기념하며!
u-ri-ŭi man-nam ŭl gi-nyŏm-ha-myŏ!

In celebration/commemoration of our meeting (= relationship)!

41 당신은 저의 첫사랑이에요.
dang-shin ŭn jŏ-ŭi chŏt-sa-rang i-e-yo.

You are my first love.

42 사랑해요.
sa-rang-hae-yo.

I love you.

43 저도 사랑해요.
jŏ-do sa-rang-hae-yo.

I love you, too.

44 제가 훨씬 더 많이 사랑해요.
je ga hwŏl-sshin dŏ man-i sa-rang-hae-yo.

I love you so much more (than you do).

45 집에까지 데려다 줄게요.
jib-e gga-ji de-ryŏ-da jul-gge-yo.

(Lit) I'll take you to home.

46 보고 있어도 보고 싶어요.
bo-go i-ssŏ-do bo-go ship-ŏ-yo.

(Lit) I miss you even though I'm looking at you.

= The more I see you the more I miss you.

47 같이 있고 싶어요.
ga-chi it-go ship-ŏ-yo.

I want to be together (= with you).

48 함께 있으면 행복해요.
ham-ggae i-ssŭ-myŏn haeng-bok-hae-yo.

(Lit) I'm happy if I'm together (= with you).

49 당신은 저에게 큰 의미입니다.
dang-shin ŭn jŏ-e-ge kŭn ŭi-mi ip-ni-da.

(Lit) You are a great meaning to me.

= You mean a lot to me.

50 제 인생에 와주셔서 감사해요.
je in-saeng e wa-ju-shŏ-sŏ gam-sa-hae-yo.

Thank you for coming into my life.

51 우리 사랑 영원히!
u-ri sa-rang yŏng-wŏn-hi!

Our love forever!

52 이 순간이 영원했으면 좋겠어요.
i sun-gan i yŏng-wŏn-hae-ssŭ-myŏn jo-ke-ssŏ-yo.

I wish this moment could last forever.

53 저희 사진 좀 찍어주시겠어요?
jŏ-hi sa-jin jom jjig-ŏ-ju-shi-get-ssŏ-yo?

Could you take a photo of us, please?

54 우리 셀카찍어요!
u-ri sel-ca jjig-ŏ-yo!

We should take a selfie!

55 좋은 꿈 꿔요.
jo-ŭn ggum ggwŏ-yo.

Have a sweet dream.

56 잘 자요, 내 사랑!
jal ja-yo, nae sa-rang!

Sleep well, my love!

57 우리는 잘 어울리지 않는 것 같아요.
u-ri nŭn jal ŏ-ul-li-ji an-nŭn gŏt gat-a-yo.

(Lit) I think we don't look good together.

58 우리는 너무 다른 것 같아요.
u-ri nŭn nŏ-mu da-rŭn gŏt gat-a-yo.

I think we are too different.

59 그만 만나는게 좋을 것 같아요.
gŭ-man man-na-nŭn-ge jo-ŭl gŏt gat-a-yo.

(Lit) I think it'd be good to stop seeing each other anymore.

60 앞으론 연락하지 말아요.
ap-ŭ-ron yŏl-lak ha-ji mal-a-yo.

(Lit) Please don't contact me from now on.

61 서로에게 짐이 되는 것 같아요.
sŏ-ro e-ge jim i doe-nŭn gŏt gat-a-yo.

I think we are being a burden to each other.

62 예전 같지 않아요.
ye-jŏn gat-ji a-na-yo.

It's not the same as before.

63 더 좋은 사람 만나길 바래요.
dŏ jo-ŭn sa-ram man-na-gil ba-rae-yo.

Hope you meet someone better.

131

Chapter 21. FAMILY

01 저희 가족을 소개합니다.
jŏ-hi ga-jog ŭl so-gae-hap-ni-da.

Let me introduce my family.

02 저희 부모님이세요.
jŏ-hi bu-mo-nim i-se-yo.

(These) are my parents.

03 많이 닮았죠?
man-i dal-mat-jyo?

We look alike a lot, right?

04 정말 똑같아요.
jŏng-mal ttok-gat-a-yo.

Really the same.

05 아빠와/엄마와 판박이네요.
a-bba wa / ŏm-ma wa pan-bag-i ne-yo.

You're the spitting image with (= of) your father/mother.

06 행복해 보이는 가족이에요.
haeng-bok-hae bo-i-nŭn ga-jog i-e-yo.

That's a happy-looking family.

07 모두 사이 좋아보여요.
mo-du sa-i jo-a-bo-yŏ-yo.

Everybody seems to get along (with each other).

08 저희 형/누나입니다.
jŏ-hi hyŏng / nu-na ip-ni-da.

(This is) my older brother/older sister.

09 몇살 차이인가요?
myŏt sal cha-i in-ga-yo?

(Lit) What age difference is it?

= What's the age difference?

10 형이 저보다 세살 많아요.
hyǒng i jǒ bo-da se sal man-a-yo.

(Lit) (My) brother is three years more than me.

11 부모님이 많이 엄하세요.
bu-mo-nim i man-i ǒm-ha-se-yo.

(My) parents are very strict.

12 대가족이죠.
dae-ga-jog i-jyo.

It's a big family.

13 저는 외동이에요.
jǒ nǔn oe-dong i-e-yo.

I am an only child.

14 사랑을 많이 받고 자랐어요.
sa-rang ǔl man-i bat-go ja-ra-ssǒ-yo.

(Lit) I grew up receiving a lot of love.

15 별로 안 닮았어요.
byǒl-lo an dal-ma-ssǒ-yo.

We don't look alike that much.

16 누가 동생인지 맞춰보세요.
nu-ga dong-saeng in-ji mat-chwǒ-bo-se-yo.

(Lit) Try guessing who is the younger sibling.

= Guess who's younger.

17 얘기 많이 들었어요.
yae-gi man-i dǔl-ǒ-ssǒ-yo.

(Lit) I've heard a lot of stories.

= I've heard a lot about you.

18 정말 사랑스러운 가족이네요.
jǒng-mal sa-rang-sǔ-rǒ-un ga-jog i-ne-yo.

It's a really lovely family.

19 화목해 보입니다.
hwa-mok-hae bo-ip-ni-da.

It seems harmonious.

20 형제들 사이 좋아보여요.
hyǒng-je-dǔl sa-i jo-a-bo-yǒ-yo.

(Your) siblings seem to get along.

21 부모님께서는 이혼하셨어요.
bu-mo-nim gge-sǒ-nǔn i-hon ha-shǒ-ssǒ-yo.

(My) parents got separated/divorced.

22 아버지는/어머니는 재혼하셨어요.
a-bǒ-ji nǔn / ǒ-mǒ-ni nǔn jae-hon ha-shǒ-ssǒ-yo.

(My) father/mother got remarried.

23 저는 입양되었어요.
jǒ nǔn ib-yang doe-ǒ-ssǒ-yo.

I was adopted.

24 자주 다퉈요.
ja-ju da-twŏ-yo.

(We) fight often.

25 뭐니뭐니해도 집이 최고죠.
mwŏ-ni-mwŏ-ni-hae-do jib i choe-go-jyo.

(Lit) When all is said and done, home is the best.

= There's no place like home.

26 엄마가/아빠가 보고싶어요.
ŏm-ma ga / a-bba ga bo-go-ship-ŏ-yo.

I miss (my) mom/dad.

27 부모님께서는 개방적이세요.
bu-mo-nim gge-sŏ-nŭn gae-bang-jŏg i-se-yo.

(My) parents are open-minded.

28 가족 전통이 있나요?
ga-jok jŏn-tong i it-na-yo?

Do you have a family tradition?

29 명절동안 제사를 지냅니다.
myŏng-jŏl dong-an je-sa rŭl ji-naep-ni-da.

We serve jesa during the holidays.

30 제사가 뭐죠?
je-sa ga mwŏ-jyo?

What is jesa?

31 돌아가신 조상님들께
인사를 드려요.
dol-a-ga-shin jo-sang-nim-dŭl gge
in-sa rŭl dŭ-ryŏ-yo.

(We) pay respect to our ancestors who passed away.

32 정말 훌륭한 전통이네요.
jŏng-mal hul-lyung-han jŏn-tong i-ne-yo.

That's a really great tradition.

33 저도 참여해보고 싶어요.
jŏ do cham-yŏ hae-bo-go ship-ŏ-yo.

(Lit) I want to try participating, too.

All right guys, now that you've learned the basic elements of Korean, you can fine-tune your Korean with our other titles focusing on different subject matter! Here are some of our best selling titles our readers love.

SPEAKING

LET'S SPEAK KOREAN

Learn over 1,400 Expressions Quickly and Easily w/ Pronunciation & Grammar Guide Marks.

Just Listen, Repeat, and Learn! Each expression comes with free downloadable MP3 files recorded by a native Korean speaker!

BEGINNERS

WRITING PRACTICE

EASY LEARNING FUNDAMENTAL KOREAN WRITING PRACTICE BOOK

GRAMMAR WORKBOOK

KOREAN FOR EVERYONE

Complete Self-Study Program : Beginner Level: Pronunciation, Writing, Korean Alphabet, Spelling, Vocabulary, Practice Quiz With Audio Files

LET'S STUDY KOREAN

Complete Practice Workbook for Grammar, Spelling, Vocabulary and Reading Comprehension w/ Over 600 Questions!

READING COMPREHENSION

ESSENTIAL KOREAN READING COMPREHENSION WORKBOOK

Multi-level practices for Beginners to Advanced

VOCAB BUILDER

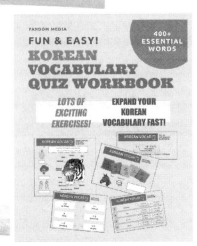

KOREAN CULTURE

QUICK & EASY KOREAN VOCABULARY

1,000 Essential Words and Phrases w/ Pronunciation Guide

FUN & EASY KOREAN VOCABULARY QUIZ WORKBOOK

Learn 400+ Essential Words w/ Exciting Exercises

KOREAN CULTURE DICTIONARY

From Kimchi to K–Pop and K–Drama Cliches. Everything About Korea Explained!

K–POP / KOREAN SLANG

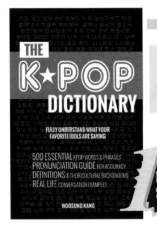

THE K–POP DICTIONARY

Fully Understand What Your Favorite Idols Are Saying

500 Essential K–Pop Words & Phrases

Pronunciation Guide

Definitions

Real Life Examples

Available in Spanish, Russian, Bulgarian, and Indonesian!